CHOICE AND CIRCUMSTANCE

CHOICE AND CIRCUMSTANCE

Racial Differences in Adolescent Sexuality and Fertility

Kristin A. Moore
Margaret C. Simms
Charles L. Betsey

Transaction Books
New Brunswick (U.S.A.) and Oxford (U.K.)

Published by Transaction, Inc., 1986.

Library of Congress Catalog Number: 85-20836
ISBN: 0-88738-062-X (cloth)
Printed in the United States of America

Library of Congress Cataloging in Publication Data

Moore, Kristin A.
    Choice and circumstance.

    Bibliography: p.
    1. Afro-American adolescent mothers.   2. Afro-American youth—Sexual behavior.   3. Adolescent mothers—United States.   4. Youth—United States—Sexual behavior.   5. Birth control—United States.   I. Simms, Margaret C.   II. Betsey, Charles L.   III. Title.
HQ759.4.M65   1986   306.7′088055   85-20836
ISBN 0-88738-062-X

This book is based on research conducted at The Urban Institute and funded by The Ford Foundation. The opinions expressed here are the sole responsibility of the authors and do not necessarily represent the views of The Ford Foundation or of The Urban Institute and its sponsors.

Contents

Foreword

Teenage childbearing affects families from all socioeconomic, ethnic, and racial backgrounds. Coping simultaneously with the tasks of childrearing, completing her education, and entering adulthood can be challenging for any adolescent mother regardless of her background or the resources and supports available to her. However, early childbearing disproportionately disadvantages black youth and their families. More than four in ten black young women have at least one child during their teenage years, accounting for a significant proportion of the growth of black households headed by women over the last two decades.

Teenage pregnancy and the growth of single-parent families in the black community can be viewed from a number of perspectives. Some see the problem as a result of a bankrupt welfare system, others as a moral problem, still others as the inevitable consequence of institutionalized racism and lack of opportunity for both black men and black women. Most agree, however, about its negative economic consequences: more than 70 percent of black children in families headed by women grow up in poverty. This statistic compels us to look more closely at the dynamics of early childbearing and ask why young black and white women take such different paths toward adulthood.

It is this question that Kristin A. Moore, Margaret C. Simms, and Charles L. Betsey address in the volume that follows. The authors carefully examine a series of factors that might be expected to contribute to differential rates of pregnancy and childbearing among black and white youth. Do black and white teenagers differ in their sexual behavior and their knowledge about how to prevent pregnancy? Do they have differential access to family planning services and do they use these services more or less effectively? And, perhaps most importantly, do black and white youth differ significantly in their goals for themselves in the areas of education, employment, and marriage and family? Do these aspirations offer differential ''protection'' against unwanted pregnancy in the light of other intervening life experience among black youth such as disproportionately poor school performance and high dropout rates and limited employment prospects? How do racial differences in marriage patterns and perceptions of community norms about out-of-wedlock childbearing affect teenage sexual behavior?

These questions are not easily answered. The authors do an outstanding job of organizing existing data from a variety of disciplines in a framework that maximizes their ability to address the questions. They also raise some provocative and important questions that broaden the focus of the debate. For example, what can we learn from the experience of young black women who manage to negotiate adolescence without bearing children?

While the complexity of the questions and significant gaps in the existing research literature prevent the authors from reaching definitive conclusions in many areas, the volume includes a set of tentative recommendations for programs and policies designed to decrease unwanted childbearing among teenagers. These recommendations and the analysis on which they are based come at a time when church and community leaders, program operators, educators, policy makers, and families themselves are asking what can be done to address the problem. The subject of teenage pregnancy has recently received significant attention among a number of black civil rights and social organizations. This volume should contribute to the plans and strategies that are generated by this promising development.

The interaction of race, class, and sex is extremely complex. This complexity is compounded by racism, sexism, and cultural stereotypes that have made it difficult to take a dispassionate look at the pattern and dynamics of adolescent childbearing in different communities. Moore, Simms, and Betsey provide us with a timely volume that summarizes the existing state of knowledge in the area and raises stimulating questions for further research and action. The Ford Foundation is extremely pleased to have been able to support this work.

Prudence Brown
The Ford Foundation

Acknowledgements

Numerous scholars, policymakers, co-workers, friends, and family have contributed to various stages of this project. A few deserve special mention. Thanks go to the high school students who participated in our interviews and the staff who made their participation possible. The help of Darryl Himes and Karen Pittman as interviewers was invaluable, as was the assistance of Leanor Johnson in designing the survey, interviewing, and reviewing early drafts.

The time and effort given by a number of outside reviewers is greatly appreciated. Martha Burt, Joy Dryfoos, Frank Furstenberg, Robert Hill, Sandra Hofferth, and Eleanor Holmes Norton all provided thoughtful and helpful comments.

A report like this one would never appear without the hard work of support staff. Carolyn Taylor O'Brien and Catherine Choisser provided research and bibliographic assistance. Bobbie Mathis cheerfully typed the many tables and drafts regardless of other pressures on her, and Terri Murray and Rosalind Fonville incorporated numerous additions and updates into the final manuscript.

Finally, the role of Prudence Brown of the Ford Foundation in initiating and guiding this project merits recognition and appreciation.

The authors hope that the integration of several disparate literatures will be helpful to other researchers and program planners. The project was a collaborative effort; however, Kristin A. Moore took primary responsibility for the chapters on information, services, and marriage and family; Margaret C. Simms took primary responsibility for the chapter on education; and Charles L. Betsey took primary responsibility for the chapter on occupational plans, job training and fertility. Our literature search suggests that many research gaps exist and we are hopeful that our colleagues will join us in attempting to further our understanding of this important topic.

Executive Summary

By the time they turn 20, 8 out of 20—41 percent—young black women already have at least one child. Among whites, only one in five teens—19 percent—has a child. In 1980, 48 percent of first births among blacks occurred to women not yet 20, compared to 25 percent among whites. In addition, births to young blacks are more likely to take place outside of marriage. Eighty-six percent of the births to black teens occurred to unmarried mothers, compared to 33 percent among whites. In all, of 156,146 births to black teens in 1980, 133,729 were out of wedlock. Among whites, 131,128 out-of-wedlock births occurred out of a total of 392,229 births. Thus, in terms of absolute numbers teenage childbearing is common among both blacks and whites; however, as a proportion of all births, early and out-of-wedlock childbearing is more common among blacks. In fact, American blacks have higher fertility than do teenagers in any other developed nation.

Evidence suggests that teenage parents and their families experience significant economic and social disadvantages. Given a slack labor market, high rates of poverty among female-headed families, and ever-higher educational requirements for today's jobs, teenage mothers and their children often have great difficulty developing their economic and personal well-being. The higher rates of early childbearing among American blacks have aroused particular concern about this issue in the black community.

To explore the factors underlying this difference in the incidence of early childbearing, an organizing framework was defined involving three sets of influences: (1) information, (2) services, and (3) aspirations. A number of studies by researchers in varied disciplines were examined regarding racial differences in information about sex and reproduction; family planning and abortion services; and aspirations in the areas of education, employment, and marriage.

Information

While most teens seem to understand the basic facts of reproduction, large gaps in understanding of pregnancy risk, contraception, and the consequences of early pregnancy exist for white as well as black teens. However, young teens, blacks, males, and teens with less well-educated parents seem to have the least knowledge. While provision of sex education in the home might be optimal, few parents seem willing or able to provide accurate and full information; the schools seem best situated to provide such teaching. Sex education should involve more than the presentation of facts, however. Approaches that involve training in decision-making skills and that help students think through their life goals and consider the effect of an early pregnancy on those goals seem most promising.

Services

It is estimated that about half of both black and white sexually experienced teens receive medical family planning services. Whites are more likely to visit a private physician, while blacks are more likely to attend a clinic; however, only half of each group is served. Young teens who have sex are less likely to use contraception, and the earlier initiation of sex among black teens seems to be a factor placing black youth at greater risk of pregnancy. Delayed and inconsistent use of contraceptives is common among both blacks and whites, and while efforts to increase the availability and accessibility of family plannning services are important, even greater emphasis should be placed on getting teens who are having sex to use available services.

High rates of sexual activity and poor use of contraception result in more than 450,000 abortions to U.S. teenagers annually. Among every age group, abortion rates are higher among black women, reflecting their higher incidence of unwanted pregnancy. Among teens, the abortion rate among blacks is twice that of whites. Despite this, some evidence indicates that there is a substantial unmet demand for abortion and that blacks are disproportionately in need of more available services. However, in view of the extremely high incidence of abortion among U.S. teens currently, high priority is not given to making abortion more available. It is concluded that higher priority should be given to efforts to reduce the incidence of unwanted pregnancy.

Education

A number of researchers have found that teenagers with high educational aspirations are more likely to delay sexual activity, pregnancy, and parenthood. The possibility that whites have higher educational aspirations than blacks and that such a difference accounts for black teens' higher pregnancy rates was explored and discounted. Youth with higher aspirations are less likely to become parents as teens among black youth and white youth alike. Studies indicate that blacks and whites have equally high educational aspirations. However, blacks are more likely to drop out of school than whites, and dropouts are more likely to become pregnant than teens who remain in school. Also, among teens in school, blacks are more likely to become pregnant and this often causes them to drop out. In terms of recommendations, it does not seem necessary to encourage black youth to raise their educational aspirations; but efforts are needed to help them achieve their already high aspirations.

Occupational Aspirations

Studies of employment plans and childbearing among teens are few in number, especially for males. Some rather weak evidence supports the notion that youth with higher aspirations delay childbearing; but it seems that the impact of an early birth on subsequent occupational status is more clear to adults than to teens. Other evidence suggests that participants in job training programs, especially females, have lower subsequent fertility. While young mothers are less likely to participate in job training programs and less likely to benefit immediately when they do participate, programs focusing on teen mothers do report lower fertility among participants than among similar young mothers not enrolled in a program.

Marriage and Family

Marriage patterns have changed greatly in the United States over the past decade among whites and blacks; however the trends are most visible among blacks. Among black women in 1982, there was no age category in which a majority of women were married and living with their husbands. In addition, blacks delay marriage later than whites, and a majority of black infants are born outside of marriage—55 percent in 1980.

Although some evidence would suggest that blacks value marriage highly, their attitudes about marriage sometimes differ significantly from those of whites. In fact, a minority of black youth prefer to begin childbearing before their preferred age at marriage. Black teenagers perceive greater tolerance for out-of-wedlock childbearing in their neighborhood than white youth, and are more accepting of premarital sexual activity. Youth from single-parent families appear to be more likely to be sexually active and to become pregnant, and since a majority of black youth are not raised by two parents, black youth are relatively disadvantaged in this regard.

Conclusions and Recommendations

Many of the factors found independently to predict early childbearing— less information, more poorly educated parents, school dropout, poor employment prospects, single-parent families—are found to be concentrated in those neighborhoods in which black children are particularly likely to be growing up. The aggregate influence of these separate factors may be greater than the simple sum of the separate effects.

A number of policy recommendations are made, including better sex education, sex education being broadly defined to include decision-making skills as well as instruction in "the facts of life"; greater availability of contraception; efforts to clarify for youth the connection between their educational and occupational aspirations and early childbearing; and efforts to assist black youth and their families to implement their already high academic and employment aspirations. Finally, it is recommended that researchers study families who are rearing their children in neighborhoods of poverty, crime, and disorganization and who yet manage to encourage abstinence or contraceptive use as they raise their children in a seemingly overwhelming environment. There are successes, and it seems important to identify which factors in families and their communities enable them to succeed and then to build on those factors.

1

Introduction

The negative medical, social, and economic consequences of teenage child-bearing have been convincingly documented. Young mothers are more likely to have babies with low birth weights and health problems (National Center for Health Statistics, 1982). School-age parents have a particularly high risk of dropping out of school (Card and Wise, 1978; Moore et al., 1978). They also tend to have larger families than women who delay childbearing (Card and Wise, 1978; Trussell and Menken, 1978; Millman and Hendershot, 1980) and teens who marry are at higher risk of marital disruption (Moore and Waite, 1981; Card and Wise, 1978). Consequently the families of teen parents have fewer earners and lower income but more children to be supported. For all of these reasons, women who first give birth as teenagers are more likely to raise their families in poverty (Hofferth and Moore, 1979). Children born to unmarried mothers are particularly likely to grow up in poverty (Bane and Ellwood, 1983). The families established by teenage mothers are also more likely to be on welfare. Over half of all the families receiving Aid to Families with Dependent Children (AFDC) are headed by women who were teenage mothers (Moore, 1978).

The effects of an early birth are not uniform by race. For example, young black mothers are more likely to have low-birth-weight babies than are white mothers (National Center for Health Statistics, 1982), while white school-age mothers are more likely to drop out of school because of a birth than are young blacks (Moore and Waite, 1978; Mott and Maxwell, 1981). Despite these differences, childbearing at young ages poses a strain to most families and to the young parents themselves, regardless of race or social status.

The fertility of white teenagers in the United States is a source of concern because of the rapid increase in early sexual activity and pregnancy documented over the last decade among whites (Zelnik and Kantner, 1980; Moore and Burt, 1982), because out-of-wedlock birth rates among white teens have risen each year almost without exception during the past ten years (National Center for Health Statistics, 1983), and because the fertility of white U.S. teenagers is considerably higher than in most other Western industrialized nations (Westoff, Calot, and Foster, 1983). Fertility rates among black teens in the United States have actually fallen slightly during the past decade (Na-

1

tional Center for Health Statistics, 1983). However, in absolute terms, black teens in the United States have higher fertility than white teenagers; indeed, they have higher rates than teenagers in any other developed nation. By the time they turn 18, nearly one-quarter of young black women are already mothers compared to less than 10 percent of whites (see Table 1.1). Nearly a third of young black women are mothers by their nineteenth birthday and more than four in ten have had a child by the time they turn 20. By age 20, less than one in five white women have had a child.

The significance of teenage childbearing to the black community has received increasingly wide recognition in recent years. One of the most eloquent leaders on this issue has been Eleanor Holmes Norton. In her words (Norton, 1983):

> I am speaking of a silent, poignant explosion of our dearest and most wonderful creatures, the infants who are the future of the black nation and of the nation as a whole. But ever increasing proportions of these are babies born with their futures tragically compromised by the high risks against their chances for success in life and even their chances for survival. These babies, blood of our blood, the descendants of nearly twenty generations of black people in America, are today often born not of women but of girls locked still in the naivete and the helplessness of their own childhood.

> These figures would be easier to bear if our strong extended family tradition had survived more often. Extended families are not uncommon in the black community today, but their incidence is much lower than it was for example, in the rural South of our historic roots. The extended family has been assaulted by the hardships of urban ghetto life, by anti-family welfare requirements and

TABLE 1.1
First Births per 1,000 Women, Cumulated to Successive Ages, Women Born 1950–1954 and 1955–1959, by Race

Age	Women Born 1950 to 1954			Women Born 1955 to 1959		
	All Races	Whites	Blacks	All Races	Whites	Blacks
18	89	68	239	94	75	223
19	153	126	354	155	130	320
20	230	200	456	220	189	413
21	299	268	525	--	--	--
22	363	331	597	--	--	--
23	421	390	648	--	--	--
24	471	443	681	--	--	--
25	526	501	711	--	--	--

Note: Rates are cumulated up to the beginning of each year, e.g., up to 18.0 for age 18.
Source: U.S. Bureau of the Census, "Childspacing among Birth Cohorts of American Women: 1905 to 1959," Current Population Reports, Series P-20, No. 385, Table 1.

by the tendency of modern American life to atomize individuals into ever smaller units. The marvelously protective extended family units that were as strong among blacks as among any group in this country are not widespread enough today to give the children of young and poor single mothers the chance they must have for a decent life.

We are of course aware that family destabilizing forces have been at work in America-at-large on the white family structure and on white teenage pregnancy rates as well. But although the numbers among whites have grown even more rapidly, they are still small in relation to the number of whites as a whole and do not constitute nearly the clear and certain danger to their community as they do to ours . . . Whether we look at this trend by itself or in comparison with whites, it must be regarded as a natural catastrophe in our midst, a threat to the future of black people without equal. What it could mean quite starkly is that with the next generation, we could see proportionately greater numbers of disadvantaged people than in this generation because of the proportion of children who got their start in life as the children of disadvantaged single girls and women.

An Organizing Framework

How can this issue be addressed? Obviously a problem of this magnitude does not lend itself to simple solutions. Human behavior is very complex, and the occurrence of a birth is the culmination of many decisions. Teenagers make decisions, whether implicitly or explicitly, regarding sexual intercourse, contraception, pregnancy, abortion, marriage, and adoption; and different factors can have different influences at different points in the process. Moreover, blacks, like whites and Hispanics, are not homogeneous. Different individuals, families, and communities hold different attitudes and values.

To sort through this complexity, we have defined an organizing framework that involves three sets of influences: (1) information, (2) services, and (3) aspirations. Each category can of course be subdivided and refined; but the categories are useful in that they highlight the contrasting types of approaches one can take to the issue of teenage pregnancy.

Providing information about sex, pregnancy, and contraception is an approach that is commonly recommended in the hope that teenagers will use this knowledge to avoid pregnancy. Most proponents of sex education realize, of course, that mere information is not sufficient. Unless teenagers abstain from sexual intercourse, services are also necessary in order to prevent pregnancy. One role that can be served by sex education is that of encouraging teens to delay sex; but for those teens who become sexually active, birth control services are needed.

During the past decade, contraception has become more widely available to teenagers; but many teenagers have failed to use contraception or have used methods sporadically. Given increased sexual activity without compensating increases in contraceptive use, pregnancy rates have risen (Zelnik and Kantner, 1980; Moore and Burt, 1982). Consequently, the number of abortions obtained by teens has risen over the past decade. Perhaps these trends are due to insufficient information and services, which would suggest that better and more widely available sex education and birth control are needed. Perhaps a lack of motivation or aspirations is also part of the problem.

A motivated young person, we suggest, can overcome barriers to information and services. The young person who is not motivated can overlook even readily available information and services. Of course, services have to be reasonably accessible and some information is necessary—that intercourse results in pregnancy and that birth control can prevent pregnancy, for example. Thus these three sets of factors influence one another. To further complicate the issue, it must be noted that there are many sources of motivation, including aspirations for schooling, employment plans, or a desire for children within marriage. We posit that aspirations for schooling, work, and childbearing within marriage will lead to delayed childbearing.

Motivation for Postponing Parenthood: Hypotheses

School enrollment and motherhood are both demanding activities and are difficult to combine. Many young mothers find it impossible to continue with their schooling. We expect the reverse to hold as well—youth who wish to continue their education tend to postpone parenthood. Therefore, a teenager's educational and occupational aspirations are hypothesized to affect her fertility behavior. Specifically, if a teenager has high aspirations she may be more motivated to take precautions to prevent pregnancy. This motivation may be tempered, however, if the individual has low expectations that she will be able to achieve her goals or faces high barriers to fulfilling her goals. If this hypothesis holds, then it could explain some of the differences between blacks and whites since there are differences in the array of opportunities available to young black and white women.

Education

Higher educational plans are expected to lead to a desire to delay childbearing because of the difficulty of combining childrearing with school enrollment. Both activities are time intensive, such that attending school and doing homework compete with child care for time and energy. In addition, attending school rarely represents a source of income, particularly below the college level. The need for income to support a family is likely to create pressure for a young person to leave school. Similarly, the need to spend money on schooling argues for postponing parenthood. Finally, high educational aspirations typically reflect high occupational aspirations, which also require postponement of childbearing. This hypothesis is expected to hold more strongly for females since childrearing burdens more often fall on the mother than the father. It should hold for males to the extent that fathers alter their lives in case of pregnancy, by marrying, by getting a job, and/or by sharing in child care.

Occupation

Higher occupational aspirations for both sexes and, for young women, planning to work steadily or pursue a career are also expected to lead to later childbearing. This should occur because child care places heavy demands on time and energy. Thus childrearing competes with the need to develop human capital through involvement in formal schooling, including both college and post-secondary vocational and technical courses, as well as on-the-job training. Because the conflict between child care and employment responsibilities tends to be greater for women, this hypothesis may hold primarily for females. A girl with low career aspirations or whose aspirations imply or require motherhood (e.g., homemaking as an aspiration) may not feel a need to defer parenthood; however, the schooling and training needs of her husband may necessitate postponement. On the other hand, particularly poor occupational opportunities—low wages, poor fringe benefits, lack of job security—may lead to more frequent out-of-wedlock childbearing if couples find it economically impossible to marry.

Marriage and Family

In addition to educational and occupational aspirations, the desire to wait until marriage before having sex or before having a child can motivate teens to abstain from sex or otherwise avoid pregnancy. The absence of marriage expectations or the general acceptance of having a child before marriage would tend to undermine this as a source of motivation. Strong values opposing sexual activity or parenthood outside of marriage are hypothesized to both reduce the incidence of premarital sex and to increase the frequency of marriage when premarital sex results in pregnancy. This occurs because the presence of such values means social disapproval will be high for those who ignore community values. Family and friends of the couple will monitor dating activities to prevent pregnancy and will encourage or insist on marriage (or possibly abortion) and may facilitate marriage (through economic or other types of support) if pregnancy occurs. Given the difficulty of monitoring sexual behavior, the effect of community values on young people's attitudes should also be a factor. If social disapproval of early, premarital sex is high and marriage is enforced for infractions, young people themselves are expected to hold attitudes that lead them to abstain from sex or to resolve pregnancy in marriage. The effect of family and community values is expected to be

6   Choice and Circumstance

stronger when resources to implement those values are greater, e.g., when income is higher and there are two parents in the home.

The absence of strong values opposing premarital sex and out-of-wedlock childbearing is expected to affect males primarily, since social and economic penalties for premarital pregnancy have traditionally been transmitted to males indirectly via marriage (though child support payments may play a similar role in the future). In the absence of marriage expectations, occupational and educational expectations of males may not affect their fertility behavior.

Why Don't More Adolescents Have Children?

Historically, early childbearing has been accepted and even encouraged in many cultures. In many developing countries, early marriage and family formation are still common (Hartley, 1975). Since most American adolescents are physically mature by their middle teen years, sexual union and reproduction are possible; yet most high school age teens abstain from sex and avoid parenthood. Why do they delay? This is, of course, the reverse of the question usually asked, which focuses on why teens do have sex and become pregnant.

We reverse the question because, for most people, pregnancy is achieved differently than other achievements. Typically, one must strive and exert effort to achieve a goal. In the case of pregnancy, one must exert effort *not* to become pregnant, either by abstaining from sexual activity or by regularly practicing effective contraception. In the absence of motivation, or when motivation is low, the likelihood of sexual activity and pregnancy are relatively high. Therefore, we suggest that it may be more fruitful to consider which teens postpone sex and pregnancy and why. Furthermore, we suggest that many teens have good reasons for postponing their sexual debut, and that it is the absence of these reasons that contributes to early sexual activity and pregnancy on the part of many teens.

The role that we envision for these motivating factors is that they provide the "push" many teenagers need to get them to resist peer pressure, obtain information, locate contraceptive services, and use birth control consistently. If information is difficult to obtain, if services are costly, if birth control is difficult to use, and if peer pressure for sex is intense, then aspirations need to be high to enable teens to overcome these barriers to pregnancy prevention.

On the other hand, if motivation is low, then even modest barriers to services or information may mean that the teen does not avail himself or herself of what is available. If aspirations are nil, even readily available services may be ignored. For example, the material presented in a sex education class may be ignored and contraceptives obtained by a friend or relative may go unused. Thus even if the barriers to pregnancy prevention are essentially removed, some teenagers can still be expected to ignore the information and services and become pregnant.

This does not imply that lowering barriers to pregnancy prevention is useless, since lower barriers mean fewer teens are likely to encounter barriers higher than their motivation. It does mean, however, that some unintended pregnancies will occur no matter how accessible services and information are made, simply because some time or effort is inevitably required to obtain and use information or birth control, and even these minimal barriers may represent too high an obstacle for some. This can be expected to be true in any society. Because different young people have more to lose objectively and subjectively due to an adolescent pregnancy, their motivation to prevent that pregnancy should vary to some extent along with the degree of loss—the cost. The question considered in this paper, however, is whether the kinds of motivation necessary to prevent early pregnancy vary by race in the United States and might therefore explain race differences in early childbearing. It is our hypothesis that they do. The occupational, educational, and marriage opportunities of black teenagers and their family backgrounds are quite different from those of white teenagers. To the extent that these factors differ by race, we hypothesize that rates of adolescent fertility will also vary by race. Fertility levels vary by social and economic status as well, and socioeconomic status is strongly correlated with race. Although our focus is on race, not socioeconomic status, and we attempt to separate the two insofar as is possible, this effort is handicapped by the fact that few studies consider race and social status simultaneously.

To explore our several hypotheses, we have reviewed existing statistics and literature relating education (chapter 5), employment (chapter 6), and marriage (chapter 7) with teenage fertility. We also interviewed a small sample of black high school students to explore some of our hypotheses in greater depth. Reflecting our expectation that information and services are also important, we have also reviewed the literature on teenagers' sex information and attitudes (chapter 3) and on birth control and abortion services for teens (chapter 4). First, though, an overview of teenage fertility is presented in chapter 2.

2

A Review of Fertility Data

Teenage and Nonmarital Childbearing

Early and out-of-wedlock childbearing are more common among black Americans than among white Americans. This statement holds regardless of the fertility measures that are used and despite shortcomings in existing measures. It has held for many years and, despite some convergence in birth rates over the past decade, the magnitude of the differences remains very large. Since this striking difference is the starting point for this paper, we have prepared a number of tables depicting varied relevant measures.[1]

Teenage Childbearing

Table 2.1 depicts the number of births to teenagers during the past several decades, by the age and race of the teenage mother. Within the youngest age group, blacks have consistently borne the majority of babies, although they represent only a minority of the population. In 1982, the most recent year for which detailed data are available, blacks under 15 had 5,395 babies, compared to 4,153 among whites. In addition, it can be seen that blacks account for nearly all of the nonwhite babies born to young mothers, since they had 96 percent of the 5,620 babies born to nonwhites.

It should also be noted, however, that the number of babies born to teenage mothers has declined among both blacks and whites over the past decade (see Table 2.2). Between 1970 and 1982, blacks registered a 19 percent decline and whites a 23 percent decline in the number of births to young women under 20. However, in both years blacks accounted for a disproportionate number of all births to U.S. teens. In 1970, blacks accounted for 27 percent of the births to women under the age of 20; in 1982, they accounted for 28 percent.

Information on the absolute numbers of births by race is important for assessing the magnitude of early motherhood and trends in the incidence of early childbearing. However, for purposes of comparison across groups, it is more appropriate to use rates, since a rate takes account of the different numbers of blacks and whites in the population.

9

TABLE 2.1
Estimated Number of Out-of-Wedlock Births in the United States, by Age of Mother, 1955–1982: Females under Twenty, by Race

Year	All Races			Whites			Nonwhites			Blacks[a]		
	Under 15	15-17	18-19	Under 15	15-17	18-19	Under 15	15-17	18-19	Under 15	15-17	18-19
1982	9,773	181,162	332,596	4,153	115,869	242,079	5,620	65,293	90,517	5,395	60,282	80,252
1981	9,632	187,397	339,995	3,970	120,913	249,100	5,662	66,484	90,895	5,425	61,850	81,428
1980	10,169	198,222	353,939	4,171	127,657	260,401	5,998	70,565	93,538	5,793	65,966	84,387
1979	10,699	200,137	349,335	4,402	127,970	255,837	6,297	72,167	93,498	6,139	67,728	85,077
1978	10,772	202,661	340,746	4,512	130,957	249,103	6,260	71,704	91,643	6,068	71,182	83,684
1977	11,455	213,788	345,366	4,671	138,223	253,960	6,784	75,565	91,406	6,582	71,182	84,008
1976	11,928	215,493	343,251	5,054	139,901	253,374	6,874	75,592	89,877	6,661	71,429	82,507
1975	12,642	227,270	354,968	5,073	148,344	261,785	7,569	78,926	93,183	7,315	74,946	86,098
1974	12,529	234,177	361,272	5,053	152,257	267,895	7,476	81,920	93,377	7,291	77,947	86,483
1973	12,861	238,403	365,693	4,907	153,416	271,417	7,954	84,987	94,276	7,778	81,158	87,615
1972	12,082	236,641	379,639	4,573	150,897	283,089	7,509	85,744	96,550	7,363	82,217	90,132
1971	11,578	226,298	401,644	4,130	143,806	302,920	7,448	82,492	98,724	7,264	79,238	92,446
1970	11,752	223,590	421,118	4,320	143,646	319,962	7,432	79,944	101,156	7,274	76,882	94,944
1969	10,468	201,770	402,884	3,684	128,156	306,118	6,784	73,614	96,766	6,650	71,020	94,944
1968	9,504	192,970	398,342	3,114	121,166	305,336	6,390	71,804	93,006	6,312	69,594	87,986
1967	8,593	188,234	408,211	2,761	118,035	317,204	5,832	70,199	91,007	5,742	68,133	86,410
1966	8,128	186,704	434,722	2,666	119,800	345,312	5,462	66,904	89,410	5,370	64,922	84,818
1965	7,768	188,604	402,290	2,444	124,294	319,460	5,324	64,310	82,830			
1964	7,816	196,220	389,490	2,676	134,596	309,762	5,140	61,624	79,728			
1963	7,594	180,564	405,890	2,584	112,096	321,212	4,814	54,848	75,662			
1962	7,340	172,836	427,462	2,690	117,660	342,172	4,520	51,818	75,970			
1961	7,462	177,894	423,826	2,808	125,194	346,512	4,654	52,700	77,314			
1960	6,780	182,408	404,558	2,524	129,544	328,586	4,256	52,864	75,972			
1959	6,776	177,786	393,262	2,572	125,822	319,548	4,204	51,964	73,714			
1958	6,648	171,786	382,418	2,648	121,704	310,992	4,000	50,062	71,426			
1957	6,960	170,716	379,496	2,648	120,040	308,934	4,312	50,676	70,562			
1956	6,356	160,580	359,842	2,348	112,184	290,638	4,008	48,396	69,204			
1955	5,883	149,722	334,375	2,136	103,503	269,175	3,747	46,219	65,200			

aData for blacks separately are not available prior to 1969.

Source: National Center for Health Statistics, Vital Statistics of the United States, annual volumes.

TABLE 2.2
Number of Births to Women under Age 20 in 1970 and 1982, by Race

	All Races		Whites		Blacks	
	Number	Decline	Number	Decline	Number	Decline
1982	523,531	20%	362,101	23%	145,929	19%
1970	656,460		467,928		179,100	

Sources: National Center for Health Statistics, "Advance Report of Final Natality Statistics, 1980," vol. 31, no. 8, November 30, 1982; and vol. 33, no. 6, September 28, 1984.

Table 2.3 presents birth rates over the past several decades by age and race. Clear declines are recorded for teenage blacks and for older whites over this period. Only a very slight decline can be noted for whites aged 15 to 17, though, while whites under 15 have shown a slight increase. Nevertheless, rates remain significantly higher among blacks, and the younger the age the greater the discrepancy. Thus in 1982, the birth rate of black teens compared with white teens was nearly twice as high among teens 18 to 19, nearly three times as high among teens 15 to 17, and seven times as high among teens under age 15. It is important to note, as well, that the black birth rate is only one-third higher among women in their early twenties and is essentially the same as the white rate through the late twenties and early thirties. Black rates are somewhat higher for those over age 35, but the major differences are found in the youngest age groups.

Given the high incidence of early childbearing among blacks, it is not surprising that teenagers account for a large proportion of all black births and particularly of all black first births, compared to whites (see Table 2.4). Again the proportion of total births accounted for by teenagers has fallen among both whites and blacks but remains considerably higher among blacks. In absolute terms, the proportion is really very high among blacks. Nearly half of black first births occur to mothers not yet 20; nearly one-quarter occur to mothers 17 and younger. One in four black infants is born to a mother under age 20, while one in eight is born to a mother 17 and younger. Hence, the pattern of high rates at young ages is one of the primary factors distinguishing black from white fertility rates. The marital status of the mothers is the other most significant difference.

Births to Unmarried Women

Data on the total number of births conceals an important difference between black and white teenagers, the proportion of births occurring out of wedlock.

TABLE 2.3
Birth Rates by Age of Mother and Race of Child, 1950–1982
(Births per 1,000 Women)

Year and Race of Child	10-14 Years	15-19 Years Total	15-17	18-19	20-24 Years	25-29 Years	30-34 Years	35-39 Years	40-44 Years	45-49 Years
All races										
1982	1.1	52.9	32.4	80.7	111.3	111.0	64.2	21.1	3.9	0.2
1981	1.1	52.7	32.1	81.7	111.8	112.0	61.4	20.0	3.8	0.2
1980	1.1	53.0	32.5	82.1	115.1	112.9	61.9	19.8	3.9	0.2
1979	1.2	52.3	32.3	81.3	112.8	111.4	60.3	19.5	3.9	0.2
1978	1.2	51.5	32.2	79.8	109.9	108.5	57.8	19.0	3.9	0.2
1977	1.2	52.8	33.9	80.9	112.9	111.0	56.4	19.2	4.2	0.2
1976	1.2	52.8	34.1	80.5	110.3	106.2	53.6	19.0	4.3	0.2
1975	1.3	55.6	36.1	85.0	113.0	108.2	52.3	19.5	4.6	0.3
1974	1.2	57.5	37.3	88.7	117.7	111.5	53.8	20.2	4.8	0.3
1973	1.2	59.3	38.5	91.2	119.7	112.2	55.6	22.1	5.4	0.3
1972	1.2	61.7	39.0	96.9	130.2	117.7	59.8	24.8	6.2	0.4
1971	1.1	64.5	38.2	105.3	150.3	134.1	67.3	28.7	7.1	0.4
1970	1.2	68.3	38.8	114.7	167.8	145.1	73.3	31.7	8.1	0.5
1965	0.8	70.4	--	--	196.8	162.5	95.0	46.4	12.8	0.8
1960	0.8	89.1	--	--	258.1	197.4	112.7	56.2	15.5	0.9
1955	0.9	90.3	--	--	241.6	190.2	116.0	58.6	16.1	1.0
1950	1.0	81.6	--	--	196.6	166.1	103.7	52.9	15.1	1.2
White										
1982	0.6	44.6	25.2	70.8	105.9	110.3	63.3	20.0	3.5	0.2
1981	0.5	44.6	25.1	71.9	106.3	111.3	60.2	18.7	3.4	0.2
1980	0.6	44.7	25.2	72.1	109.5	112.4	60.4	18.5	3.4	0.2
1979	0.6	43.7	24.7	71.0	107.0	110.8	59.0	18.3	3.5	0.2
1978	0.6	42.9	24.9	69.4	104.1	107.9	56.6	17.7	3.5	0.2
1977	0.6	44.1	26.1	70.5	107.7	110.9	55.3	18.0	3.8	0.2
1976	0.6	44.1	26.3	70.2	105.3	105.9	52.6	17.8	3.9	0.2
1975	0.6	46.4	28.0	74.0	108.2	108.1	51.3	18.2	4.2	0.2
1974	0.6	47.9	28.7	77.3	113.0	111.8	52.9	18.9	4.4	0.2
1973	0.6	49.0	29.2	79.3	114.4	112.3	54.4	20.7	4.9	0.3
1972	0.5	51.0	29.3	84.3	124.8	117.4	58.4	23.3	5.6	0.3
1971	0.5	53.6	28.5	92.3	144.9	134.0	65.4	26.9	6.4	0.4
1970	0.5	57.4	29.2	101.5	163.4	145.9	71.9	30.0	7.5	0.4
1965	0.3	60.7	--	--	189.8	158.8	91.7	44.1	12.0	0.7
1960	0.4	79.4	--	--	252.8	194.9	109.6	54.0	14.7	0.8
1955	0.3	79.1	--	--	235.8	186.6	114.0	56.7	15.4	0.9
1950	0.4	70.0	--	--	190.4	165.1	102.6	51.4	14.5	1.0
Black										
1982	4.1	97.0	71.2	133.3	139.1	106.9	60.4	24.4	5.4	0.4
1981	4.1	97.1	70.6	135.9	141.2	108.3	60.4	24.2	5.6	0.3
1980	4.3	100.0	73.6	138.8	146.3	109.1	62.9	24.5	5.8	0.3
1979	4.6	101.7	75.7	140.4	146.3	108.2	60.7	24.7	6.1	0.4
1978	4.4	100.9	75.0	139.7	143.8	105.4	58.3	24.3	6.1	0.4
1977	4.7	104.7	79.6	142.9	144.4	106.4	57.5	25.4	6.6	0.5
1976	4.7	104.9	80.3	142.5	140.5	101.6	53.6	24.8	6.8	0.5
1975	5.1	111.8	85.6	152.4	142.8	102.2	53.1	25.6	7.5	0.5
1974	5.0	116.5	90.0	158.7	146.7	102.2	54.1	27.0	7.6	0.6
1973	5.4	123.1	96.0	166.6	153.1	103.9	58.1	29.4	8.6	0.6
1972	5.1	129.8	99.5	179.5	165.0	112.4	64.0	33.4	9.8	0.7
1971	5.1	134.5	99.4	192.6	186.6	128.0	74.8	38.9	11.6	0.9
1970	5.2	147.7	101.4	204.9	202.7	136.3	79.6	41.9	12.5	1.0
1965	4.3	140.6	--	--	247.8 .	183.2	114.9	62.7	18.7	1.4
1960	4.3	156.1	--	--	295.4	218.6	137.1	73.9	21.9	1.1

Source: National Center for Health Statistics, *Vital Statistics of the United States*, annual volumes.

TABLE 2.4
Percentage of U.S. First Births and All Births in Which the Mother's Age Was
under 20 or 18, by Race

	All Races				Whites				Blacks[a]			
	First Births (%)		All Births (%)		First Births (%)		All Births (%)		First Births (%)		All Births (%)	
Year	≤17	<20	≤17	<20	≤17	<20	≤17	<20	≤17	<20	≤17	<20
1982	11	26	5	14	8	23	4	12	23	45	11	25
1980	11	28	6	16	9	25	5	14	26	48	12	26
1975	16	35	8	19	13	31	6	16	32	57	16	33
1970	14	36	6	18	11	32	5	15	32	59	15	31
1965	14	38	5	16	11	35	4	14	33	59	12	22
1960	14	37	4	14	12	24	4	13	30	54	9	20
1955	12	31	4	12	9	28	3	11	28	51	8	20
1950	10	27	4	12	8	24	3	10	28	50	9	21

[a]Percentages for the years 1950, 1955, and 1960 pertain to nonwhites rather than blacks due to insufficient data on live black births.
Source: National Center for Health Statistics, calculated from Vital Statistics of the United States, annual volumes.

Among younger blacks, the number of out-of-wedlock births is nearly as high as the total number of births, reflecting the fact that nearly all births among young black teenagers take place outside of marriage. Among blacks altogether, 57 percent of all births occurred outside of marriage in 1982. Among black teens, 87 percent of all births occurred outside of marriage. High as these proportions are, they may be underestimates since all births to separated women are tabulated as marital births. At 38 percent, the proportion of births that are out of wedlock is also high among white teens, but the contrast with black teens is so striking that it almost makes the white proportion seem low in comparison.

As shown in Table 2.5, the number of out-of-wedlock births increased among both blacks and whites over the 1970s. However, the magnitude of the increase has been far greater among whites—65 percent among 15- to 19-year-old unmarried whites between 1970 and 1982 compared to 13 percent among comparable blacks. Nevertheless, the number of out-of-wedlock births

TABLE 2.5
Number of Births in the United States by Age of Mother, 1955–1982: Females under Twenty, by Race

Year	All Races			Whites			Nonwhites			Blacks[a]		
	Under 15	15–17	18–19	Under 15	15–17	18–19	Under 15	15–17	18–19	Under 15	15–17	18–19
1982	8,720	117,696	142,930	3,225	57,848	72,829	5,495	59,848	70,101	5,305	56,608	65,555
1981	8,589	118,608	140,631	3,030	57,881	71,105	5,559	60,727	69,526	5,361	57,882	65,601
1980	9,024	121,900	140,877	3,144	57,761	70,223	5,880	64,139	70,654	5,707	61,204	66,818
1979	9,500	120,000	133,000	3,300	54,300	62,100	6,200	65,900	70,900	6,100	62,900	67,100
1978	9,400	116,500	123,200	3,300	52,500	55,900	6,100	64,000	67,300	5,900	61,200	64,000
1977	10,100	120,900	118,700	3,400	53,800	53,200	6,700	67,100	65,500	6,500	64,400	62,700
1976	10,300	116,500	108,500	3,500	50,000	47,600	6,800	66,500	60,900	6,600	64,100	58,600
1975	11,000	116,800	105,800	3,600	48,900	45,000	7,500	67,900	60,700	7,200	65,500	58,200
1974	10,900	113,000	97,700	3,300	44,800	40,300	7,300	68,300	57,500	7,700	66,100	55,100
1973	10,900	111,300	93,500	3,200	42,400	38,700	7,700	69,000	54,800	7,500	67,000	52,900
1972	9,900	108,500	93,700	2,700	39,900	38,700	7,200	68,600	55,100	7,100	66,700	53,200
1971	9,500	100,800	93,200	2,500	36,200	39,900	7,100	64,700	53,500	6,900	63,100	51,800
1970	9,500	96,100	94,300	2,500	36,200	43,200	7,000	60,000	51,100	6,800	58,400	49,500
1969	8,300	83,300	84,900	2,100	30,800	39,500	6,200	52,500	45,300	6,100	51,200	43,800
1968	7,700	77,900	80,200	1,900	28,400	38,900	5,800	49,500	41,200			
1967	6,900	70,900	73,500	1,700	24,800	35,500	5,200	46,100	38,000			
1966	6,200	65,900	69,800	1,400	23,400	34,100	4,800	42,500	35,800			
1965	6,100	61,700	61,400	1,400	21,500	29,200	4,600	40,200	32,200			
1964	5,800	58,700	52,700	1,400	21,600	23,600	4,400	37,100	29,100			
1963	5,400	51,100	50,700	1,200	17,900	21,900	4,000	31,800	27,500			
1962	5,100	46,100	48,300	1,300	15,500	20,700	3,800	29,700	26,600			
1961	5,200	45,100	48,100	1,400	15,500	20,600	3,800	29,600	27,500			
1960	4,600	43,700	43,400	1,200	15,000	17,800	3,500	28,700	25,600			
1959	4,600	43,100	41,500	1,200	14,400	16,500	3,400	28,600	25,000			
1958	4,400	40,100	39,300	1,200	13,200	15,300	3,300	26,900	24,000			
1957	4,600	39,400	37,100	1,100	12,500	14,400	3,500	26,900	22,700			
1956	4,200	37,000	35,900	1,000	11,400	13,900	3,200	25,600	22,000			
1955	3,900	34,700	34,200	900	10,600	13,100	3,000	24,200	21,100			

[a]Data for blacks separately are not available prior to 1969. Blacks included among nonwhites in all years.

Source: National Center for Health Statistics, Vital Statistics of the United States, annual volumes.

to whites has only recently come to approach the number among blacks, even though whites represent a majority of the population.

Table 2.6 presents data for the past decade on the incidence of childbearing to unmarried women by age and race. As noted above, unmarried women

TABLE 2.6
Out-of-Wedlock Birth Rates, by Age of Mother, 1970–1982; by Race
(births per 1,000 unmarried females in age group)

| | | Age of Mother | | | | |
| | 15-19 Years | | | | | |
	Total	15-17 Years	18-19 Years	20-24 Years	25-29 Years	30-34 Years
Whites						
1982	17.7	12.9	25.1	25.7	22.2	14.7
1981	17.1	12.4	24.6	24.9	21.6	13.6
1980[a]	16.2	11.8	23.6	24.4	20.7	13.6
1980[b]	16.0	11.8	23.1	22.6	17.3	10.3
1979	14.6	10.8	21.0	20.3	15.9	10.0
1978	13.6	10.3	19.3	18.1	14.8	9.4
1977	13.4	10.5	18.7	17.4	14.4	9.3
1976	12.3	9.7	16.9	15.8	14.0	10.1
1975	12.0	9.6	16.5	15.5	14.8	9.8
1974	11.0	8.8	15.3	15.0	14.7	9.5
1973	10.6	8.4	14.9	15.5	15.9	10.6
1972	10.4	8.0	15.1	16.6	16.5	12.1
1971	10.3	7.4	15.8	18.7	18.5	13.1
1970	10.9	7.5	17.6	22.5	21.1	14.2
Blacks						
1982	87.0	67.6	115.8	110.2	85.5	45.8
1981	86.8	66.9	117.6	112.5	86.4	47.2
1980[a]	89.2	69.6	120.2	115.1	83.9	48.2
1980[b]	93.5	74.2	123.9	115.3	79.5	43.4
1979	91.0	71.0	123.3	114.1	80.0	44.8
1978	87.9	68.8	119.6	111.4	79.6	43.9
1977	90.9	73.0	121.7	110.1	78.6	45.7
1976	89.7	73.5	117.9	107.2	78.0	45.0
1975	93.5	76.8	123.8	108.0	75.7	50.0
1974	93.8	78.6	122.2	109.8	80.3	51.8
1973	94.9	81.2	120.5	116.0	84.5	57.8
1972	98.2	82.8	128.2	121.2	88.3	57.4
1971	98.6	80.7	135.2	130.6	99.6	68.6
1970	96.9	77.9	136.4	131.5	100.9	71.8

[a]Rate calculated using new methodology for assessing marital status in states not reporting on marital status. See Vol. 31, no. 8. These methodological changes at National Center for Health Statistics in definition of out-of-wedlock births are responsible for nearly half of the increase in the rate among whites between 1979 and 1980 shown in this rate.
[b]Rate calculated using same methodology used in earlier years.

Sources: Monthly Vital Statistics Report, summary report—natality statistics, vol. 33, no. 6; vol. 32, no. 9; vol. 31, no. 8; vol. 23, no. 3; vol. 22, no. 7; 1970 Vital Statistics, "Trends on Illegitimacy—U.S., 1940–1965," U.S. Department of Health, Education, and Welfare, February 1968, Table 2.

are those who are never married, divorced, or widowed; separated women
are combined with women who are married and living with their husbands.[2]
   Considering out-of-wedlock birth rates among teenagers in Table 2.6, it is
clear that the rates are far higher among blacks. Among teens 18 to 19, the
out-of-wedlock birth rate is more than four times higher among blacks compared to whites. It is more than five times higher among teens aged 15 to
17. It should be noted that the rate was slightly lower among blacks in the
early 1980s than in the early 1970s, while it has risen rather steadily among
whites. Nevertheless, convergence in the rates of whites and blacks is not in
sight for women in any age group. Even among women over 20, the differences are so great that they cannot be explained by data errors. In addition,
these same differences have been noted by other investigators using different
data (Hofferth 1983; O'Connell and Rogers, 1982), and while important
differences related to social and economic status can be noted, race differences
do not disappear when several measures of social and economic status are
controlled.
   O'Connell and Rogers (1982) have analyzed data from the Current Population Survey on out-of-wedlock childbearing by race, family income, and
education of the woman. As shown in Table 2.7, the out-of-wedlock birth
rate is higher among black women aged 18 to 44 than among white women,
even within income and educational groupings. Of course, the groupings are
quite broad, so there is undoubtedly variation within the categories. For
example, within an income group such as $5,000 to $9,999, black families
are likely to be more concentrated in the lower portion of the range. Never-

TABLE 2.7
Births Per 1,000 Unmarried Women Ages 18–44, by Race, June 1981

	White Women	Black Women
Family Income ($)		
Under 5,000	44.1	117.1
5,000–9,999	35.3	63.5
10,000–19,999	11.3	34.9
Over 20,000	8.6	48.3
Education		
Not a high school graduate	51.4	92.7
High school, 4 years	17.6	72.8
College, 1 year or more	5.8	34.0

Source: M. O'Connell and C. Rogers, "Out of Wedlock Childbearing: Trends and Differentials," 1982, Tables 7, 8.

theless, the magnitude of the difference is so great that it is unlikely that somewhat finer categories would eradicate the differences.

Data on the proportion of births to women that occurred out of wedlock show a similar pattern such that black rates are higher even within categories of education and income (see Table 2.8). It should be noted that the incidence of out-of-wedlock childbearing does vary according to the educational and income measures; the point is that racial differences remain even when the large social and economic differences between blacks and whites are statistically controlled to some extent. The magnitude of the differences that remain suggest a real difference or real differences between black and white fertility patterns that reflects more than just racial differences in economic status. They may well be related to the social and economic status of blacks in American society but they are not likely to be identified simply as a function of differential status.

Hispanic Fertility

Recent data from the Current Population Survey also provide an opportunity to explore early childbearing among Hispanics compared to whites and blacks. Among mothers aged 30 to 34 in 1980, the percentage who were less than 20 when their first child was born was 54 percent among blacks, 33 percent among whites, and 30 percent among mothers of Spanish origin[3] (Bureau of the Census, 1982, Table 18). Data on younger women suggest, though, that

TABLE 2.8
Percentage of All Births That Occur to Unmarried Women Ages 18–44, by Race, Family Income, and Education, June 1981

	White Women (%)	Black Women (%)
Family Income ($)		
Under 5,000	32.0	70.1
5,000–9,999	20.3	39.7
10,000–19,999	5.1	33.3
Over 20,000	4.0	25.6
Education		
Not a high school graduate	19.6	57.7
High school, 4 years	8.0	45.9
College, 1 year or more	3.8	30.0

Source: M. O'Connell and C. Rogers, "Out of Wedlock Childbearing: Trends and Differentials," 1982.

fertility among the Spanish-origin population is or has become higher than fertility among whites (see Table 2.9).

Other data from the Current Population Survey suggest that Hispanics achieve a high proportion of their expected fertility while yet quite young (see Table 2.10). In each case, the figure for Hispanics is intermediate between the figures for blacks and whites. The number of children expected by these groups of women varies little. However, the relatively high levels of fertility among young black and Spanish-origin women indicate that greater effort

TABLE 2.9
Births to Date per 1,000 Women, by Ethnicity and Marital Status, June 1981

	White	Black	Spanish Origin[a]
All Women			
18 - 19	148	450	269
20 - 21	373	847	637
22 - 34	665	1,304	1,054
Never Married Women			
18 - 19	46	408	102
20 - 21	83	742	383
22 - 24	123	1,060	526

[a]Persons of Spanish origin may be of any race.
Source: U.S. Bureau of the Census, Fertility of American Women: June 1981, 1983, Current Population Reports, Series P-20, No. 378, Table 2.

TABLE 2.10
Percentage of Lifetime Births Expected Already Born, by Age of Woman and Ethnicity, June 1980

	White		Black		Spanish Origin[a]	
	Total (%)	Single (%)	Total (%)	Single (%)	Total (%)	Single (%)
Age of Woman						
18 - 19	8.8	2.5	24.1	21.4	18.6	8.6
20 - 21	18.1	2.9	42.7	37.4	28.5	9.1

[a]Persons of Spanish origin may be of any race.
Source: U.S. Bureau of the Census, "Fertility of American Women: June 1980, 1982," Current Population Reports, Series P-20, No. 375, Table 2.

will be necessary for these young women to avoid exceeding their expected level of fertility, or that their fertility expectations are too'low. It should be noted that, although Spanish-origin women as a group have achieved a substantial proportion of their total expected fertility by their early twenties, single Spanish-origin women have achieved only 9 percent of their expected fertility, compared to a figure of 37 percent among single black women and 3 percent among single white women. Thus it seems clear that the early childbearing that does occur among Hispanics tends to be marital childbearing.

Differences in the Process Leading to Teenage Parenthood

What is the source of these racial differences in the teenage fertility rate? Exploration of this question is, of course, the goal of this study. However, this question can be asked and answered in a purely demographic and descriptive sense, and it is necessary to do so before pursuing it in a larger sense.

Differences exist between blacks and whites at each step in the process of becoming a teenage parent. Blacks are more likely to have premarital sexual intercourse, more likely to become pregnant given that they have had sex, slightly more likely to have an abortion (in recent years) given that they have become pregnant, less likely to marry given that they have the baby, and less likely to give the child up for adoption given that they bear an out-of-wedlock child. These differences will be described in the following sections, prior to proceeding with a more detailed consideration of the reasons for these differences.

Sexual Activity and Fecundity

Numerous researchers have found black teenagers more likely to have had sexual intercourse at a given age (e.g., Bauman and Udry, 1981). The definitive data on this question are from the series of three national surveys conducted in 1971, 1976, and 1979, shown in Table 2.11. At each age in each survey, black females are more likely to have had premarital coitus, and the mean age at first intercourse is nearly a year younger among black females.

Since black females 14 and younger seem to be slightly more fecund than comparable whites (Harlan et al., 1980), those who become sexually active are at greater risk of pregnancy. Earlier maturity may hasten sexual activity as well, of course; however differences in fecundity seem too small to explain the large racial difference in the frequency of early, premarital intercourse.

Only one national survey of male sexual activity is currently available. Differences among males by race, shown in Table 2.12, are not nearly as striking; however, the males who were interviewed in the 1979 Kantner/

TABLE 2.11
Percentage of Women Age 15–19 Who Ever Had Intercourse before Marriage, by Marital Status and Race

Marital Status and Age	1979			1976			1971		
	Total	White	Black	Total	White	Black	Total	White	Black
All									
%	49.8	46.6	66.2	43.4	38.3	66.3	30.4	26.4	53.7
N	1,717	1,034	683	1,452	881	571	2,739	1,758	981
Ever-married									
%	86.7	86.2	91.2	86.3	85.0	93.9	55.0	53.2	72.7
N	146	106	40	154	121	33	227	174	53
Never-married[a]									
Total	46.0	42.3	64.8	39.2	33.6	64.3	27.6	23.2	52.4
15	22.5	18.3	41.4	18.6	13.8	38.9	14.4	11.3	31.2
16	37.8	35.4	50.4	28.9	23.7	55.1	20.9	17.0	44.4
17	48.5	44.1	73.3	42.9	36.1	71.0	26.1	20.2	58.9
18	56.9	52.6	76.3	51.4	46.0	76.2	39.7	35.6	60.2
19	69.0	64.9	88.5	59.5	53.6	83.9	46.4	40.7	78.3
Age at First Intercourse (all)									
Mean	16.2	16.4	15.5	16.1	16.3	15.6	16.4	16.6	15.9
Number	933	478	455	726	350	376	936	435	501

[a]Sample sizes are not shown for each single year of age in order to simplify the presentation: N ≥ 87 for each age-race cell among the never-married.

Note: Figures refer to the household population of SMSAs. Base excludes those for whom no information was obtained on premarital intercourse. Percentages are computed from weighted data. ''White'' includes the relatively small number of women of races other than black. Except where indicated, the base excludes those who did not respond to the question analyzed in the table. Absolute numbers shown are unweighted sample numbers.

Source: M. Zelnik and J. Kantner, ''Sexual Activity, Contraceptive Use and Pregnancy among Metropolitan-Area Teenagers: 1971–1979,'' *Family Planning Perspectives* 12(1980), Table 1.

Zelnik study were older than the females and any racial differences that might have been apparent in a younger sample would not appear in these data.

Pregnancy

Sexual activity does not automatically lead to pregnancy, of course. Fecundity is one factor that affects the probability of conception and, as noted, data suggest that black females are somewhat more fecund than whites at younger ages; but the differences seem to be slight past the age of 14 (Harlan et al., 1980). The use of contraception strongly reduces the probability of pregnancy among young couples, as it does among older couples.

TABLE 2.12
Percentage of Men Ages 17–21 Who Ever Had Intercourse before Marriage,
by Marital Status and Race, 1979

Marital Status and Age	Total	White	Black
All			
%	70.3	69.6	74.6
N	(917)	(567)	(350)
Ever-married			
%	82.7	83.3	72.8
N	(74)	(58)	(16)
Never-married[a]			
Total	68.9	67.8	74.7
17	55.7	54.5	60.3
18	66.0	63.6	79.8
19	77.5	77.1	79.9
20	81.2	80.7	85.7
21	71.2	68.0	89.4

[a]N ≥ 33 for each age-race cell among the never-married.

Source: M. Zelnik and J. Kantner, "Sexual Activity, Contraceptive Use and Pregnancy among Metropolitan Area Teenagers: 1971–1979," *Family Planning Perspectives* 12(1980), Table 2.

Data from the Kantner/Zelnik surveys indicate that black teenagers are more likely to never use contraception (see Table 2.13). Moreover, even within categories of contraceptive use, blacks are more likely to become pregnant (see Table 2.14). The exception to this statement occurs among teenagers who report that they have always used contraception; in this case blacks are slightly less likely to have experienced a pregnancy. However, the overwhelming majority of pregnancies reported occurred to those who never used a contraceptive or who irregularly used a contraceptive, and black teens in each of these categories experience considerably higher probabilities of pregnancy (see Table 2.14).

Overall, black teens are considerably more likely to become pregnant than are white teens, even when pregnancy rates are calculated just among sexually active teens. The contrast is demonstrated in Table 2.15, which presents estimates of the pregnancy rate among teenagers by race using two different methodologies. The top panel reports the proportion ever-pregnant from Zelnik and Kantner's 1979 National Survey of Young Women (1980, Table 3). Since underreporting of abortion is a problem for studies based on personal interviews, a second estimate is presented that is calculated from data on births

TABLE 2.13

Percentage Distribution of Premarital Sexually Active Women Ages 15–19, by
Contraceptive-Use Status, According to Race

Contraceptive Use Status[a]	1979			1976		
	Total (N=937)	White (N=478)	Black (N=459)	Total (N=724)	White (N=349)	Black (N=375)
Always used	34.2	35.0	31.2	28.7	28.9	28.0
Used at first intercourse but not always	14.7	16.1	9.7	9.5	10.1	8.1
Did not use at first intercourse but used at some time	24.5	24.9	23.3	26.3	28.6	20.2
Never used	26.6	24.0	35.9	35.5	32.4	43.7
Total	100.0	100.0	100.0	100.0	100.0	100.0

Note: Contraceptive use prior to pregnancy, marriage, or time of survey, whichever event
was earlier.
Source: M. Zelnik and J. Kantner, "Sexual Activity, Contraceptive Use and Pregnancy among
Metropolitan-Area Teenagers: 1971–1979," *Family Planning Perspectives* 12(1980),
Table 7.

and abortions relative to the estimated number of married and unmarried sexually
experienced teenagers. Regardless of the method employed to prepare the estimate, it is clear that pregnancy is far more common among black teens.

Abortion

In 1980, nonwhites accounted for 30 percent of all abortions. Their abortion
rate of 56.8 per 1,000 women was twice as high as the white rate of 24.3.
In addition, black women terminated 39.2 percent of all pregnancies compared
to 27.4 percent among whites (Henshaw and O'Reilly, 1983, Table 2). As
Table 2.16 shows, the abortion rate among nonwhites exceeds that among
whites at all ages. The ratio of abortions per 1,000 births to females aged 12
to 19 is only slightly higher among blacks—643 abortions per 1,000 live
births compared to 615 among whites (see Table 4.14). These data indicate

TABLE 2.14
**Premaritally Sexually Active Women Ages 15–19, by Contraceptive-Use
Status, According to Race**

Contraceptive Use Status[a]	1979			1976		
	Total	White	Black	Total	White	Black
Always used						
%	13.5	13.7	12.4	9.9	10.0	9.5
(N)	(307)	(165)	(142)	(203)	(98)	(105)
Used at first intercourse but not always						
%	31.0	26.2	59.5	39.7	34.3	57.6
(N)	(119)	(73)	(46)	(66)	(36)	(30)
Did not use at first intercourse but used at some time						
%	29.2	25.0	45.2	21.7	22.2	19.7
(N)	(241)	(137)	(104)	(171)	(95)	(76)
Never used						
%	62.2	58.8	70.3	49.5	41.5	65.2
(N)	(270)	(103)	(167)	(283)	(120)	(163)

Note: Contraceptive use prior to pregnancy, marriage, or time of survey, whichever event was earlier.

Source: M. Zelnik and J. Kantner, "Sexual Activity, Contraceptive Use and Pregnancy Among Metropolitan-Area Teenagers: 1971–1979," *Family Planning Perspectives* 12(1980), Table 8.

that the abortion rate differs more by race than does the proportion of pregnancies terminated by abortion. This is a function of the higher pregnancy rate among blacks. Blacks have a higher abortion rate than whites but because of their higher pregnancy rate, the proportion of pregnancies ending in abortion is similar for blacks and whites. This pattern holds among teenagers and older women (see Tables 4.12 through 4.14).

Marriage

Analyses of Current Population Survey data (O'Connell and Moore, 1980; O'Connell and Rogers, 1984) document a clear racial difference in the marital experience of young mothers. Black teenagers are considerably more likely to become pregnant before marriage, and are also less likely to legitimate the pregnancy by marrying before the baby's birth (see Table 2.17). The proportion of first births occurring outside of marriage and the proportion legitimated have risen dramatically among whites. However, the proportion of

TABLE 2.15
Proportion of Young Women Ages 15–19 Pregnant in 1979, by Race

		Whites	Blacks
Panel A:	Proportion of females 15 - 19 ever pregnant before marriage, for all women and for those ever having premarital intercourse, 1979		
	All females 15 - 19	13.5	30.0
	Females ever having premarital intercourse	29.0	45.4
Panel B:	Proportion of teenagers 15 - 19 pregnant in 1979, among all teenagers and among married and unmarried, sexually experienced teenagers		
	All females 15 - 19	8.1	19.4
	Sexually experienced and married females	17.1	29.0

Source: Panel A—M. Zelnik and J. Kantner, "Sexual Activity, Contraceptive Use and Pregnancy among Metropolitan-Area Teenagers: 1971–1979," *Family Planning Perspectives* 12(1980), Table 3. Panel B—Kristin A. Moore, The Urban Institute.

first births occurring before marriage has also increased among black teens, maintaining the striking racial disparity.

Out-of-Wedlock Childbearing and Adoption

The end result of the several steps described so far is, of course, the higher incidence of teenage motherhood, particularly out-of-wedlock teenage motherhood among blacks, that was depicted in Tables 2.5 and 2.6 at the beginning of this chapter.

Out-of-wedlock childbirth does not necessarily imply out-of-wedlock motherhood; however, the two appear to have become essentially the same thing in recent years as the incidence of adoption has fallen precipitously. Historically, of course, most unmarried black mothers have kept and raised their children. Only during the past decade or so have whites assumed the black pattern. Although there are no reliable national data on the frequency with which mothers relinquish their babies for adoption, it is generally accepted that "these days" most unmarried women who carry their pregnancies to term do keep and raise the child themselves regardless of their race.

Subsequent Childbearing among Teen Mothers

A number of studies have found that women who initiate childbearing at an early age tend to have relatively large families (Card and Wise, 1978;

TABLE 2.16
Abortions per 1,000 Women, by Age and Race, and Ratio of White Rate to Nonwhite Rate, 1980

Age Group	Abortion Rate White	Abortion Rate Nonwhite	Ratio of Nonwhite Rate to White Rate
Under 15	5.0	24.4	4.9
15 - 19	38.3	66.0	1.7
20 - 24	43.1	95.6	2.2
25 - 29	24.5	64.7	2.6
30 - 34	13.3	38.9	2.9
35 - 39	7.4	21.0	2.8
40 or Over	3.0	6.7	2.2

Source: S. Henshaw and K. O'Reilly, ''Characteristics of Abortion Patients in the United States, 1979 and 1980,'' Family Planning Perspectives 15(1983): 8.

Moore and Hofferth, 1978; Trussell and Menken, 1978; Millman and Hendershot, 1980). Blacks in recent cohorts have only slightly larger families than whites who began childbearing in their teen years (Trussell and Menken, 1978; Millman and Hendershot, 1980). However, the higher rate of first births among young blacks translates into a higher rate of high parity births as well. Data from the Vital Statistics systems (shown in Table 2.18) clearly indicate the higher birth rates among blacks at higher parities. Among blacks in their early twenties, a substantial majority of the births that are taking place are second or higher-order births. At higher birth orders, the proportion black is higher. As Table 2.19 shows, among all first births to teenage mothers in 1980, 72 percent of the first births were white babies. Among the fifth or later-order births, only 36 percent were white. As the data for 1968 show, this trend has held for a long time. As Fuchs (1983) notes, this is not an encouraging statistic from the point of view of blacks, since the literature documenting the privileged position of first-borns and children in small families is now extensive.

Other data indicate the clear effect of age, though not of race, on the interval between births, among women proceeding on to the next birth order (see Table 2.20). Among teenagers having a second or higher-order birth, a majority of both black and white mothers had the later birth within two years of the previous birth. Older women, both black and white, space their children much further apart. Hence it is clear that many teenage mothers compound their problems with rapid childbearing. While current cohorts of black teenage mothers do not appear more likely than whites to bear subsequent children

TABLE 2.17

Percentage of First Born Babies Conceived Out of Wedlock, by Year of Baby's Birth and Race of Mother, Females 15–19, by Marital Status at Time of Childbirth

	Birth Cohort of Baby						
	1950–1954	1955–1959	1960–1964	1965–1969	1970–1974	1975–1979	1980–1981
White Mothers Ages 15 – 19							
Single at first birth	9.4	10.6	13.7	14.5	20.2	30.3	36.8
Married at first birth	13.2	20.8	24.7	33.3	37.1	27.8	27.6
Total proportion conceived out of wedlock	22.6	31.4	38.3	47.7	57.3	58.1	64.4
Black Mothers Ages 15 – 19							
Single at first birth	46.6	52.8	62.1	61.3	75.7	83.2	87.9
Married at first birth	18.3	22.5	19.0	19.8	15.4	10.1	8.5
Total proportion conceived out of wedlock	64.9	75.3	81.1	81.1	91.1	93.4	96.5

Source: M. O'Connell and C. Rogers, "Out-of-Wedlock Births, Premarital Pregnancies and Their Effect on Family Formation and Dissolution," *Family Planning Perspectives* 16(1984): 157–62, Table 1.

shortly after the first, their higher incidence of initial child-bearing results in their being overrepresented among those having higher parity births at young ages and with short birth intervals.

Conclusions

The trends of primary concern are not all moving in the same direction. Consequently some recapitulation is appropriate. First the total number of births to teenagers has fallen among both blacks and whites; however, the number of out-of-wedlock births has increased among both blacks and whites. Similarly, the rate of births per 1,000 teens has fallen among both blacks and whites, a decline which has not been matched when the rate of nonmarital births is considered. The out-of-wedlock birth rate has fallen slightly among black teens 18 to 19, but it has not consistently fallen among younger blacks. Among white teens, the out-of-wedlock birth rate rose over the 1970s. Nevertheless, the rate is many times higher among young blacks than among young

TABLE 2.18
Birth Rates by Age of Mother, Live-Birth Order, and Race of Child, 1980
(births per 1,000 women)

| | Age of Mother | | | | |
| | | 15-19 | | | |
	10-14	15-17	18-19	15-19	20-24
All Races					
Total	1.1	32.5	82.1	53.0	115.1
First child	1.1	28.5	59.7	41.4	57.3
Second child	0.0	3.6	18.6	9.8	39.8
Third child	0.0	0.3	3.2	1.5	13.5
Fourth or later	0.0	0.0	.6	0.2	4.5
Whites					
Total	0.6	25.2	72.1	44.7	109.5
First child	0.6	22.7	54.8	36.0	57.2
Second child	0.0	2.3	15.1	7.6	37.8
Third child	0.0	0.2	2.0	0.9	11.4
Fourth or later	0.0	0.0	0.0	0.1	3.0
Blacks					
Total	4.3	73.6	138.8	100.0	146.3
First child	4.2	61.3	87.3	71.8	55.9
Second child	0.1	10.9	39.0	22.3	51.2
Third child	0.0	1.3	10.3	4.9	25.9
Fourth or later	0.0	0.1	2.1	0.9	13.4

Source: National Center for Health Statistics, *Monthly Vital Statistics Report*, vol. 31, no. 8, November 30, 1982, Table 3.

whites, and it remains higher even when social and economic differences between blacks and whites are taken into account. Birth rates among Spanish-origin youth are considerably lower than among blacks but higher than among whites. In addition, young Spanish-origin women are considerably more likely to have children within marriage relative to blacks.

Considering the origin of these differences in a purely demographic or descriptive sense, blacks and whites differ at most steps in the process of becoming a teen parent. Black youth are considerably more likely to initiate sexual intercourse at a young age, more likely to become pregnant having begun to have sex, somewhat more likely to terminate the pregnancy in abortion, substantially less likely to marry to legitimate the pregnancy, and less likely, data suggest, to relinquish the child for adoption. What factors can be identified, beyond the purely descriptive, to shed light on the reasons underlying these differences?

TABLE 2.19

Percentage Distribution of Live Births to Teenage Mothers, by Race and Birth Order

	Total	White	Nonwhite
1980			
All births	100.0	69.8	30.2
First births	100.0	71.9	28.1
Second births	100.0	64.7	35.3
Third births	100.0	51.2	48.8
Fourth births	100.0	41.2	58.8
Fifth or later births	100.0	35.5	64.5
1968			
All births	100.0	76.5	28.5
First births	100.0	74.7	25.3
Second births	100.0	63.8	36.2
Third births	100.0	48.3	51.7
Fourth births	100.0	36.7	63.3
Fifth or later births	100.0	31.0	69.0

TABLE 2.20

Percentage of Live Births by Interval since Last Live Birth, by Age of Mother and Race (43 reporting states and D.C.)

	Under 20	20-24	25-29	30-34
Whites				
1-11 months	6.0	1.9	0.9	0.7
12-17 months	30.0	14.0	7.7	5.7
18-23 months	25.2	17.2	11.9	8.8
24-35 months	28.0	29.8	24.9	18.4
$\geq$ 36 months	10.9	37.1	54.7	66.5
Percent < 2 years	61.2	33.1	20.5	15.2
Blacks				
1-11 months	6.6	3.0	1.7	1.2
12-17 months	28.5	14.6	8.6	7.1
18-23 months	23.1	14.5	8.6	7.3
24-35 months	26.5	23.4	15.9	12.5
$\geq$ 36 months	15.3	44.5	65.3	71.9
Percent < 2 years	58.2	32.1	18.9	15.6

Source: National Center for Health Statistics, "Interval between Births: United States, 1970–77," 1981, Table B.

Notes

1. Hispanic teenagers also have relatively high fertility rates. Their fertility rate is higher than that of whites but lower than that of blacks. However, information on Hispanic fertility is much less readily available, particularly for years before the 1980s. This is true for other minority groups as well, for example, Indians and Orientals. Consequently, most of the tables presented report data for just blacks and whites.

2. Births to separated women are omitted from the out-of-wedlock numerator and separated women are omitted from the out-of-wedlock denominator. This results in an overestimate of the rate of out-of-wedlock childbearing. For example, if separated women had been included in the calculations for 1975, the out-of-wedlock birth rate for blacks would have been 18 percent lower (Ventura, 1980). The effect might be larger but most out-of-wedlock births occur to never married women (Hofferth, 1983). Moreover, separated women represent a relatively small proportion of teenagers, so this bias is fairly small at the younger ages. Nevertheless, the result of this procedure may be an underestimate of the number of nonmarital births but an overestimate of the out-of-wedlock birth rate. In other words, the proportion of all births out of wedlock may be even higher among blacks than official data indicate, while the out-of-wedlock birth rates may be too high, particularly among older black women. This bias is probably minor for teens, though.

3. Persons of Spanish origin may be of any race.

3

Information and Attitudes

Some of the most troubling data on adolescent pregnancy are those indicating that most unmarried teens who become pregnant did not intend their pregnancy. Among females 15 to 19 in 1979 who reported a premarital pregnancy and who did not marry, only 21 percent of the black teenage females and 16 percent of the whites reported intending the pregnancy (Zelnik and Kantner, 1980). Why are unwanted pregnancies so common?

A reasonable starting point in exploring this issue is to consider the role of information. Perhaps teens (1) do not know how pregnancy occurs; (2) do not understand the risk of pregnancy for themselves; or (3) don't know how to prevent pregnancy or have inaccurate information regarding pregnancy prevention. Given our concern with fertility differences associated with race and ethnicity, we need to consider whether reproductive knowledge is lower among blacks and Hispanics and whether attitudes differ, and, if so, whether these differences could account for differing birth rates.

What Do Teens Know?

Few researchers have attempted to ascertain whether teenagers know "where babies come from." The common perception that even rather young teens have a general understanding of conception seems to be supported, though. In a study of preadolescent blacks in Washington, D.C., ranging in age from 8.3 to 11.4 years, only about a third seemed to have no knowledge of how conception occurs (Jenkins, 1983). Among a sample of teens making their first visit to a contraceptive clinic, only 1 percent of the sample cited "Just learned I could get pregnant if I had sex" as the major reason they had come to the clinic. Another 5 percent cited it as a contributing factor (Zabin and Clark, 1981). Our own small-scale survey of black high school students (see Table 3.1) also suggests that a lack of knowledge about conception plays only a small role in the occurrence of teenage pregnancy. Fewer than one-third of the respondents checked "they [teenagers] don't know how pregnancy happens" as even a contributing factor. Only 3 to 7 percent ranked this as one of the top three factors in explaining adolescent pregnancy. Thus it seems unlikely that very many adolescents who engage in sexual intercourse are

TABLE 3.1
Percentage of Black 9th- and 10th-Grade Students Reporting Knowledge about Conception and Contraception as a Factor or as One of Top Three Factors Explaining Why Teenagers Who Have Sex so Often Experience Pregnancy

| | Reasons Boys Have | | | | Reasons Girls Have | | | |
| | Boys' Opinions | | Girls' Opinions | | Boys' Opinions | | Girls' Opinions | |
	% Checked	% Marking Top 3	% Checked	% Marking Top 3	% Checked	% Marking Top 3	% Checked	% Marking Top 3
They don't know how pregnancy happens	26	6	31	7	24	3	31	5
They don't know about birth control (about using pills, condoms, IUD, diaphragm, withdrawal, or rhythm to prevent pregnancy)	50	11	41	11	58	14	45	12
(N)	(42)		(39)		(41)		(42)	

unaware that coitus leads to pregnancy. On the other hand, the completeness of their understanding and their comprehension of ways to keep coitus from resulting in pregnancy may be more limited.

Respondents in our survey were more likely to check lack of knowledge of birth control, compared to lack of knowledge regarding conception, as a factor contributing to pregnancy. About half of the sample checked "they [teenagers] don't know about birth control" as a contributing factor (see Table 3.1). Again though, just a little more than one in ten ranked this as one of the top three reasons. National data suggest that birth control awareness may be lower among blacks than among whites, however. Zelnik and Shah (1983) report that among women having unplanned first intercourse without contraception, 23 percent of blacks but 9 percent of whites said they did not know about contraception at that time. If not viewed as the most important reason, there are nevertheless indications that a less than full understanding of pregnancy and contraception are contributing factors. Other studies provide additional examples.

One study of 200 inner city black women—one-third of whom were teenagers, two-thirds of whom were currently pregnant, and all of whom had been pregnant—indicated that 56 percent of the women could not correctly state why women menstruate. (Many felt the process rids the body of excess blood or impurities.) In addition, 79 percent of the women did not know whether there is "a 'safe time' to have intercourse without becoming pregnant" (Poland and Beane, 1980). Presuming that all of these women understand in general how their pregnancies occurred, it nevertheless appears that they lack a full understanding of the reproductive process.

Some types of knowledge are inevitably more crucial than others; for example, perception of pregnancy risk. Many younger adolescents apparently feel they are not at risk because they are so young (Kantner and Zelnik, 1973). While this may be true for teens just entering puberty, when full fertility is attained they do become at risk of pregnancy. Apparently, though, when their initial risk-taking is successful they come to believe they are sterile. Therefore they come to believe that they don't need to contracept. Eventually, though, they become fertile and pregnancy occurs.

Women's evaluation of the risk of pregnancy given intercourse varies greatly. Miller (1976) reports that in a sample of young white women ranging in age from 17 to 26, respondents assessed the chances of pregnancy given unprotected intercourse once or twice a week over a year's time to be as low as 25 percent and as high as 100 percent. Sexually active college students with a lower subjective perception of pregnancy risk were found to have taken more contraceptive risks during the past four weeks than students who felt the odds of pregnancy to be higher (Crosbie and Bitte, 1982).

In assessing risk and taking responsibility, younger adolescents are handicapped by their cognitive immaturity (Cobliner, 1981; Cvetkovich et al.,

1975; Hatcher, 1973; see also McAnarney, 1982). Before reaching the stage of formal operational thinking, adolescents are unable to think abstractly or think about the future (Piaget, 1969), and this undermines their ability to plan for and use contraception.

Cvetkovich et al. (1975) have described several cognitive strategies common among adolescents, the personal fable and the imaginary audience. The adolescent's belief in an imaginary audience presumes that others are preoccupied with the same concerns as the adolescent. Therefore the adolescent is unable to differentiate the object of his or her own thought from that of other persons and believes that use of contraceptives would be a clear signal to others that sex was premeditated. Since the adolescent cannot admit this to him or herself or to others, contraception is precluded.

The personal fable, on the other hand, arises from the adolescent's belief that his or her own emotions, problems, and experiences are unique and that the laws of probability don't apply to them. Thus, even if they understand that pregnancy can occur the first time or if a couple only has sex once, they don't believe pregnancy will happen to them.

There are no data indicating that black teens are more likely to be handicapped by such cognitive immaturity. However, since 41 percent of black 15-year-olds compared to 18 percent of white teens the same age are sexually active (Zelnik and Kantner, 1980), it seems likely that a higher proportion of black teens are placed at risk by cognitive immaturity than is the case among whites. (Fifteen is the youngest age for which reliable national data are available.)

In addition to lesser cognitive maturity due to their early initiation of sex, young blacks are also handicapped by lower levels of literacy than whites the same age. Among 13- and 17-year-olds, for example, nonwhites have consistently scored below whites on tests of literal comprehension, inferential comprehension, and reference skills (National Assessment of Educational Progress, 1981). Such data suggest that sex education initiated by the teen or sponsored by schools or community institutions will be undercut more often among young blacks by their lesser ability to read and assimilate information.

Many types of information are relevant to pregnancy prevention. Health risks associated with contraception appear to be an important area of misinformation. Despite numerous studies indicating that the physical risks of pregnancy exceed the risks of contraception, particularly for adolescents (e.g., Ory, 1983), the belief that using birth control is harmful is widespread. Among the sample of black high school students studied by Freeman et al. (1980), 58 percent believed the pill is harmful. Ross (1979) reports that blacks cited health as a major reason for nonuse in her New York City sample. White females were less likely to be afraid of health risks. In the survey of clinic attenders studied by Zabin and Clark (1981), 8 percent cited "thought birth control dangerous" as the primary reason they delayed coming to the clinic, while 27 percent cited it as a contributing reason. Presumably, teens attending clinics are less likely to be fearful of birth control than teens in general. In our survey of black high school students, we asked students who feel problems with birth control are a factor in teenage pregnancy to indicate what kinds of problems teens have. Considering problems girls are perceived to have with birth control, 37 percent of the boys but 69 percent of the girls checked "They think birth control is dangerous." Twenty-four percent of the boys and girls alike included this among their top three reasons for teenage pregnancy.

Knowing how to use birth control is another type of relevant knowledge. Surprisingly little is known about users' and nonusers' knowledge of different methods. One question in particular has been asked by a number of researchers—the time in the menstrual cycle when pregnancy risk is greatest—and thus provides a way to consider at least one facet of this kind of knowledge. Results from six studies are presented in Table 3.2. Clearly, information on the time of greatest risk within the menstrual cycle is lacking. Data from Presser's reinterviews suggest, moreover, that many of those who initially answered correctly simply guessed the right answer.

Other data indicate that information gaps are common. Among a sample of eighth graders, for example, only half knew that a girl can get pregnant the first time she has intercourse (Parcel and Luttman, 1981). Freeman et al. (1980) report that only 44 percent of the males and 64 percent of the females in their sample of black urban teenagers agreed that "birth control needs to be used if sex is occasional."

Although studies that control for factors such as race, sex, age, and socioeconomic background simultaneously are uncommon, it is still possible to note some differences in level of knowledge among different population groups. Most clear is a sex difference with males being less knowledgeable (Jenkins, 1983; Delcampo et al., 1976; Freeman et al., 1980; Ross, 1979). Not surprisingly, older teens are better informed, as are teens whose mothers are better educated (Kantner and Zelnik, 1972). Teens who have had sex education tend to be more knowledgeable (Zelnik and Kim, 1982; Farrell et al., 1978; Parcel and Luttman, 1981). In addition, white teens tend to be better informed than black teens, even when mother's education is controlled (Kantner and Zelnik, 1972), even when both groups have had sex education, and regardless of whether or not the teen is sexually experienced (Zelnik and Kantner, 1981).

Attitudes

A variety of attitudes that are relevant to the occurrence of early pregnancy vary by race. For example, blacks interviewed in the 1976 national survey (Zelnik, Kantner, and Ford, 1981) were more likely to agree that "sex is always all right" than were whites—43 versus 19 percent among 15- to 17-

TABLE 3.2
Summary of Research Results on Reproductive Knowledge among Teenagers

Women **most** likely to become pregnant about 2 weeks after a period begins (true) Sample of 1909 teen parents on AFDC in Illinois: Child Policy Research Project, 1983	% Correct 14			

	% Correct		% Don't Know	
A woman's fertile time (when she is most likely to become pregnant) is half-way between her menstrual periods (true) Elective after-school course, 62 regular attending 8th-graders: Parcel and Luttman, 1981	Pre 42	Post 72	Pre 47	Post 15

A girl can most easily get pregnant just before her period begins (false) 421 male urban high school students: Finkel and Finkel, 1975	% Correct 46

When during the month is there the greatest risk of pregnancy? Initial interviews with 129 mothers 15-19 in New York City: Presser, 1971	% Correct 19

	% Correct in Initial and Reinterview		
When during the month is the greatest risk of pregnancy? 103 mothers interviewed twice in New New York: Presser: 1981	All Races 10	Whites 12	Blacks 9

	% Correct								
	All Races			Whites			Blacks		
Time of greatest pregnancy risk within the menstrual cycle,	all	yes	no	all	yes	no	all	yes	no
by race and whether sexually experienced	41	47	37	44	53	40	24	24	23
by race and whether had sex education National survey of young women 15-19; Zelnik and Kantner, 1981	41	45	32	44	48	37	24	26	16

year-olds. Black teenagers tend to favor a younger age at childbearing. In 1976, 35.2 percent of the black teenage females aged 15–19 favored having a first birth while under the age of 20 compared to 6.5 percent of the whites (Zelnik, Kantner, and Ford, 1981).

In another study, pregnant black teens indicated that they expected and received a less negative response from parents and particularly from peers when they revealed their pregnancy than did the pregnant white teens who were also interviewed (Williams, 1977). Similarly, black respondents aged 15 to 19 interviewed across the nation in 1976 (Zelnik, Kantner, and Ford, 1981) were considerably less likely to perceive neighborhood condemnation of an unwed mother. Fifty-nine percent of whites compared to 36 percent of blacks perceived very strong or strong condemnation. Ten percent of whites but 33 percent of blacks perceived no condemnation at all. On the other hand, when asked to consider the reaction of society in general, 55 percent of whites and 53 percent of blacks perceived very strong or strong condemnation of the unwed mother. Thus, perceptions of society in general are very similar, but black teens view their own communities as being more accepting than the larger society.

Very few studies have explored the linkages between information, attitudes, and pregnancy. Of course this is an extremely difficult enterprise. If causality is to be determined precisely, prospective data are required and then data collection over a fairly long follow-up period is necessary. Most studies have looked at more near-term outcomes expected to be associated with a reduction in pregnancy, e.g., better contraceptive use, an increase in reproductive knowledge, or development of attitudes opposed to risk-taking. Results from such studies are beginning to accumulate, however.

Sex Education in Schools and Media

Sex Education

Studies of sex education programs have tended to find that students' reproductive knowledge is increased; that students become more tolerant of other people's sexual practices; that students' own personal morality is not affected; that sexual activity is not more likely as a consequence of enrollment; and that students are more likely to support sexual responsibility, fidelity, and sexual equality as opposed to the double standard (Kirby et al., 1979; McCary, 1978; Brown, 1983; Farrell et al., 1978; Schinke et al., 1979; Gunderson and McCary, 1980). One macro-level study (using aggregate data) of sex education in large city schools reports no effect on teen fertility rates, however (Sonenstein and Pittman, 1983), and a review of a number of sex education programs (Kirby, 1983) reports little impact of these programs on teen behavior. Schinke et al. (1981), on the other hand, reports that students enrolled in sex education courses with an emphasis on decision making were better contraceptors over the next year compared to the control group.

The one micro (individual-level) analysis conducted on a national sample (Zelnik and Kim, 1982) demonstrates a fairly strong association between having had sex education that included birth control and a lower incidence of pregnancy (see Table 3.3). Teen females in each age-race group, both 1976 and 1979, reported a lower incidence of premarital pregnancy if they had had sex education. Although the researchers were not able to identify whether sex education occurred before or after initial intercourse and pregnancy, Zelnik and Kim correctly note that data on the relative timing of events

TABLE 3.3
Percentage[a] of Never-married, Sexually Active Teenage Women Who Have
Been Pregnant, by Whether They Had Had Sex Education Including
Discussion of Contraception, According to Race and Age

	1976				1979			
	White		Black		White		Black	
Sex Education Status	15-17	18-19	15-17	18-19	15-17	18-19	15-17	18-19
Had sex education	14.7	17.2	23.5	48.2	15.4	25.0	28.7[b]	49.2
(N)	(68)	(58)	(132)	(110)	(123)	(120)	(136)	(139)
Did not have sex education	21.2	30.8	36.7	53.8	25.0	31.9	49.2[b]	54.0
(N)	(33)	(26)	(30)	(39)	(44)	(47)	(61)	(63)

[a]Percentages are computed from unweighted data.
[b]$p < 0.05$.
Source: M. Zelnik and Y. Kim. "Sex Education and Its Association with Teenage Sexual
Activity, Pregnancy and Contraceptive Use," Family Planning Perspectives 14 (1982):
117-26, Table 5.

could only have strengthened the case for sex education.[1] That an effect has
been demonstrated anywhere is fairly remarkable since there are many and
varied reasons why sex education should not be expected to have a strong
impact.

Jorgensen (1981) argues that too much is expected from sex education
programs because a number of major obstacles exist that undermine the ability
of sex education programs to have an impact on pregnancy rates. He discusses
four barriers, including, first, the fact that a significant minority of teenagers
want to become pregnant; second, the lack of fit between the level and style
of adolescent thought and most sex education curricula; third, stereotypical
sex roles including male-dominated dating relationships, an orientation toward
sexual conquest, lack of male responsibility for contraception, and less com-

mitment and communication with the partner; and fourth, a lack of parental awareness of and support for contraception.

Moreover, we would assert that further formidable obstacles exist. First, the sex education that most teens receive is highly abbreviated and only infrequently has a clear, strong goal of changing behavior as well as increasing knowledge (Sonenstein and Pittman, 1983; 1984). It bears noting that most sex education programs are oriented toward education, and studies of information programs addressed at other teen behaviors such as smoking and drinking report similarly that information alone is insufficient (Polich et al., 1984). Role playing and other techniques to help adolescents resist peer pressure, develop self-esteem, and make decisions that enhance their own goals are being used increasingly, in view of the strong influence of peers on the behavior of most teens. It should also be noted that most teens are regularly exposed to permissive messages provided by the advertising and entertainment industries, which compete with the messages proferred in sex education curricula. In fact, the focus on schools as the source of sex education seems unfortunate, since practically all youth have greater exposure in terms of quantity to media influences than they do to sex education in the schools.

Media Influences

Youth at ages 11–15 interviewed in the 1981 National Survey of Children reported that they watch over four hours of television every day (Messaris and Hornik, 1983). Parent estimates from the 1976 National Survey of Children (Zill and Peterson, 1981) indicate that on average children aged 7 to 11 watch over two hours of television daily. Although black and Hispanic children do watch slightly more television than white children (124 minutes for white, 133 for black, and 151 minutes for Hispanic children), the difference is trivial relative to the large absolute level of television viewing. These data suggest that prepubertal children are exposed to over 700 hours of television annually.

Although the quantity of television viewing may not differ much by race, the content of what is viewed could vary substantially, e.g., educational television versus adult "soaps." Moreover, television is not the only source of media exposure. Radio stations and movies oriented toward teens are often highly suggestive and frequently very explicit. In addition, advertising in magazines, billboards, stores, and elsewhere often uses sex to attract interest.

It is possible that neither the quantity nor quality of media exposure is the issue. It may be that the "sexual sell" is so pervasive in American society that virtually all children and youth are exposed to it. It does seem quite possible, though, that some children are more susceptible to what they see and that family variables mediate the impact of media exposure. For example, parent communication about television programs has been found to be associated with lower levels of sexual activity regardless of the amount of television watched (Peterson, Moore, and Furstenburg, 1984).

Whether minority youth are exposed to a greater incidence of suggestive or explicit sex in movies, radio, or print has not been documented. Whether exposure leads to earlier, more promiscuous, or less considered sex has not been documented either, nor has the mediating role of the family been explored. Any statements regarding the impact of the media must be highly speculative since research on the topic is as yet very limited. This neglect of the possible role of media by researchers should be rectified. In the interim, any consideration of what school-based sex education can accomplish should be cognizant of children's regular exposure to competing messages.

Discussion

Results from several studies indicate that sex education programs can lower the risk of pregnancy for those enrolled, but the effect is often minimal and is found to be nonexistent in many studies. Courses seem to have more of an impact on knowledge than on behavior, and pregnancy is still common among teens, especially black teens, even when they have had sex education. Moreover, a causal influence has not been definitively documented.

Some might assume that it is not necessary to establish a clear causal relationship between sex education and early pregnancy; however, there are powerful reasons for documenting such a relationship, if it does exist. First, there is considerable competition for time in the school curriculum. Programs that have a demonstrated utility are more likely to receive time. Second, introducing sex education can be risky and time consuming for school administrators. There are many people who feel that sex education cannot have an overall effect in reducing pregnancy because students who take sex education are more likely to have sex in the first place, or who feel strongly that sex education belongs in the home. Administrators can naturally be expected to be less than enthusiastic about pushing for a program that poses high costs of varied types if the benefits are not certain.

Despite opinion poll data indicating fairly widespread support for sex education in the schools (Orr, 1982), a vocal and politically powerful minority believe sex education encourages promiscuity. In fact, such worries appear to be quite widespread even among people who are not explicitly opposed to sex education. For example, many parents seem to fear that if they discuss contraception with their children they will be perceived as condoning sexual activity (Furstenberg, 1971).

This is one of the most difficult issues faced by persons who seek to reduce the incidence of adolescent pregnancy by increasing the reproductive understanding of adolescents. We hypothesize that one of the chief barriers to the introduction of sex education programs in this country is the explicit conviction held by a minority of the population and the unexpressed but real concern felt by a large proportion of the population that sex education causes teens to initiate sexual activity when they otherwise would not have done so. As discussed above, the evidence to date does not suggest that those teens who receive sex education outside the family are more likely to be sexually active and it does suggest that teens who have had sex education have more knowledge and act in ways that reduce the probability of pregnancy. However, we feel that this issue of the relative costs and benefits of sex education is so significant, particularly to policy makers on the state and local level and to educators, that carefully designed longitudinal studies are warranted. We would argue that even if reproductive knowledge is not the most central determinant of adolescent pregnancy, the absence of accurate knowledge places a cap on teenagers' ability to prevent pregnancy if that is their intention. For example, teens who believe pregnancy cannot occur because they are "too young" may initiate sexual activity or have unprotected sex and only later come to learn that they were wrong. How can teens be helped to acquire such relevant information?

How Can Reproductive Knowledge of Adolescents Be Increased?

It seems clear that more than simple transmission of information is necessary. As Fisher (1983: 286) notes, sex education must "develop instructional techniques that will affect *both* knowledge and behavior." Accurate information on ways to prevent pregnancy is essentially irrelevant to a teen who desires pregnancy or who doesn't care whether pregnancy occurs. In addition, information on reproduction and contraception may be viewed as irrelevant by other youths if they do not appreciate the effect a pregnancy could have on their own lives.

To help youth appreciate cause-effect processes and develop rational decision-making skills, a number of investigators have been working on decision-making models of sex education (Schinke et al., 1981; Maracek, 1981; Maskay and Juhasz, 1983). These approaches appear particularly promising. For example, Schinke et al. (1981) report that 6, 9, and 12 months after training, groups trained in decision-making strategies were less likely to engage in unprotected intercourse, were more habitual users of birth control, and held more positive attitudes about family planning compared to control groups that had no training. These young people participated in a 14-session program using a group method guided by social workers to help youths acquire facts about reproduction and contraception and to develop problem-solving skills. Students were taught to recognize a problem, to derive a variety of solutions to problems, and to anticipate outcomes when solutions are exercised. Then, when they reached reasoned solutions about dating, sexual activity, and contraception, the youth practiced implementing their decisions in the group setting. For example, verbal and nonverbal communication skills were discussed and practiced.

Even with an approach that augments information with values clarification and training in the communication and decision-making skills necessary to translate that information into behavior, one must consider who would be the best agent for providing such schooling. We suspect that everyone's first choice would be the parents of teenagers. Reasons for such a choice undoubtedly vary greatly, from a vision of the family as the appropriate source of moral teaching, to a belief that it would be more cost effective for families rather than public institutions to provide such teaching, to the belief that parents can best tailor the timing and content of a sexual education to the developmental level of their own child, all excellent reasons.

The main problem with relying on parents is that so few have taken up the task. For a topic with as little clarity and certainty as that of sex education, one conclusion seems clear: parents, particularly fathers, do not provide a reproductive education for their children, particularly their sons (Finkel and Finkel, 1975; Fox, 1980; Freeman et al., 1980; Ross, 1979; Rothenberg, 1980). While girls are more likely to get sex education in the home, the information they get may be inaccurate and is often incomplete. Perhaps this is because parents feel overwhelmed with the pace of the sexual revolution and are unable to provide advice. Perhaps parents lack sufficient understanding themselves. Freeman et al., 1980, did find that the students with the least accurate information were those reporting the mother or sister as sources, and Zelnik, 1979, found that for black female teens the home was one of the poorest sources of information. Or, perhaps, as Fox (1980) suggests, the maturational crises experienced by parents as they grow older are exacerbated by the child's emerging sexuality, making the topic too difficult to be handled. Rothenberg (1980) reports that more than a third of the mothers in her study indicated that they did not find it easy to discuss sex with their children. Whatever the reason or reasons, parents by and large have not taken on the job of providing comprehensive sex education to their children.

Presumably programs directed toward parents could be of great assistance in making parents more knowledgeable, more self-assured, and more comfortable in dealing directly with their growing children's sexuality. Then parents could provide sex education to their children. However, questions remain. Are parents interested? Who is going to provide such training for America's parents? Will the parent with the greatest need in the eyes of his or her child or of an instructor be the parent who steps forward for a voluntary course?

We tend to agree philosophically that parental teaching is the mode of first choice. In addition, we think parents reared during the past several decades will be more involved and comfortable discussing sex when they become parents. Furthermore, many parents may seek the information or communication skills on their own, or simply be scared into action by media coverage of the issue of adolescent pregnancy. Perhaps television producers will take the initiative and provide sex education in the academic sense during the late evening hours, when parents can watch a program with or without their child. However, we cannot be sanguine that enough parents will take the initiative or that parents can always be relied on for accurate information. Nor are we optimistic that sufficient educational programs will be offered either on television or in the community. If offered it is not assured that enough parents or the parents most in need of instruction will take advantage of what is offered. Ultimately, therefore, as most people do, we must resort to recommending the schools.

It should be noted that evidence exists that a majority of urban teens now receive sex education (Zelnik and Kim, 1982) and that a majority of large city school systems now offer sex education (Sonenstein and Pittman, 1984). However, though 80 percent of city school districts offer sex education, only 16 percent of the senior high programs are recognized as separate courses and coverage amounting to six to ten hours per year is most typical. In addition, curriculum topics tended to concentrate more on the facts of body development and pregnancy and less on the decision-making, communications, and values issues that seem to be important in both making the information relevant and useful.

Many community organizations including churches are involved in providing sex education, and many of them are more innovative and cover a broader range of topics than school programs (Scales and Kirby, 1981). However, promising as these approaches are, self-selection may limit the effectiveness of such programs. Those youths in greatest need, in the perception of someone other than the youth, may be those least likely to enroll in a program offered by a voluntary community organization.

Most youths attend school, though, particularly during the junior high years. This is a time when sex education can be provided to virtually all youth before most are exposed to the risk of pregnancy. Let us reiterate, though, that we mean sex education broadly defined—that is, including discussion of life goals, training in decision making and resisting peer pressure, and introduction to the use of contraception methods.

Sex education is unlikely to be a panacea, of course. Expectations should be modest. However, as we noted above, the absence of accurate information essentially places a cap on the ability of teenagers' efforts to control their fertility. The effectiveness of sex education may be correspondingly limited by teenagers' lack of motivation to control their fertility, as we will discuss later; but some types of curricula might have the effect of creating motivation. For example, budgeting exercises may bring home the cost of maintaining a child, while caring for toddlers in a school day care center or the popular egg exercise (in which students must keep constant surveillance over an egg for a week) may bring home the realities of parenthood.

Summary and Conclusions

Teenagers are aware of the basic facts of conception and of the existence of contraception, but many gaps exist in their information. While many schools do provide sex education, coverage tends to be limited. Most parents, particularly fathers, provide little information to their growing children. Sons are particularly ignored. More detailed and accurate information, more discussion of relationships, more training in decision making, a greater awareness of peer and media influences, and training to resist social pressure are needed.

One comparison of blacks and whites based on national data suggests that blacks are less well-informed than whites, even among those who have had sex education or who have comparably educated mothers. This difference may contribute to the racial differences in the incidence of adolescent pregnancy; but it is not of sufficient magnitude to explain birth rates that differ by a factor of seven among teens under 15 and by a factor of three among teens 15 to 17.

The younger age common among blacks when they initiate sexual activity is probably a factor, since both the amount of information that a teen has acquired and the ability of the teen to process the implications of that information are less at younger ages. It is not clear exactly when teens become cognitively able to deal with the possibility of conception and to manage the task of contraception. Further research to establish an age, an age range, a percentile, or some kind of lower age limit seems necessary. If such research does establish that some age or age range is too young cognitively, then strong efforts should be initiated to encourage teens to delay sexual activity past that age.

For teens able to assimilate and integrate what they learn in sex education into their sexual activity, a need for detailed and accurate information should be recognized. The lower literacy levels of black youths probably hinder their ability to read and comprehend information about sex, pregnancy, and contraception. Readily understood information should be provided no later than junior high. However, more than just facts are needed. Coverage should include reproduction and birth control and accurate information on the relative health risks of pregnancy and birth control should be provided. In addition, the social and economic costs of early parenthood should be discussed. Developing decision-making skills and exploring life goals vis-à-vis fertility goals should also be a part of sex education. Even accurate and readily available information will not prevent pregnancy among adolescents who want to become pregnant, who do not care whether they become pregnant, or who see no connection between achieving their goals and early parenthood. In addition, sexually active teens who prefer to avoid pregnancy may face an additional obstacle if birth control services are not available and accessible. It is to this topic that we turn next.

Note

1. This occurs because some girls who were classified as having had sex education and also as being sexually experienced or as having had a premarital pregnancy actually did not take the course until after first intercourse or first pregnancy; if these cases were removed the proportion who had sex education and also reported intercourse or pregnancy would be lower.

4

Contraception and Abortion

Numerous studies have been done on the psychological and social factors associated with earlier and more regular use of effective methods of contraception (Mindick, 1980; Chilman, 1979; Zelnik, Kantner and Ford, 1981) Far fewer researchers have explored the institutional and societal factors affecting the availability and accessibility of birth control methods. Obviously, both issues are important and their influences interact. Our current concern is with the latter—the availability of birth control and abortion methods.

Following our use of the "barrier" analogy, it is our expectation that when services are less available or less accessible, a barrier to the use of birth control exists. If motivation is high, then strong efforts will be made to overcome the barriers; but if motivation is low, then even modest barriers will reduce the probability that a young person will obtain birth control methods. In this chapter, the relative availability and accessibility of birth control methods to black and white youth is discussed. We define availability and accessibility as do Moore and Burt (1982: 115):

> *Availability* of a service refers to its presence or absence in a teenager's community, and also to how much of the service is present in relation to the number of people who need it.

> *Accessibility* of a service refers to the ease with which a client can use the service. Accessibility has numerous aspects: it must be physically possible to get to a clinic or agency in a reasonable amount of time and at reasonable expense; sites must be open at times a teenager can reasonably use them (late afternoons, evenings, and weekends); it should be possible for teenagers to use the agency or clinic in a confidential way, when necessary; and financial support for services must be available for those teens who cannot themselves afford the services and who cannot turn to their parents for financial help. Finally, teenagers must know the service exists, and that it has all of these desirable properties.

We are focusing on the supply of contraception and abortion services. Are family planning services less available or accessible to black teenagers than to white teenagers? Is differential availability of birth control services a factor that accounts for the higher fertility of young blacks? Is abortion less available

47

to black than to white teens? Is differential availability of abortion a factor that accounts for higher black birth rates?

While assessing the supply of services sounds straightforward, in fact, this concept is difficult to quantify. First, the supply is to some extent responsive to the demand. That is, if a young person goes to a clinic, she or he will be served, and the supply of services will have expanded to meet the demand. In addition, services that objectively exist may not be available or accessible subjectively. For example, the location of a clinic, hours of service, the cost of services, rules regarding the display of contraceptives in drug stores, and stipulations requiring parental permission or notification are factors that affect the supply of birth control in the sense that they affect the availability and accessibility of contraception to teenagers. In addition, teenagers have to be aware of how and where they can obtain contraception. Teens may perceive barriers that in fact do not exist.

Teenagers in a New York City study (Ross, 1979) were asked "Is birth control available to teenagers in your area without lots of hassle?" Two-thirds of the teens who had not had sex responded that they did not know. Even among sexually active respondents, though, a third of the females and 41 percent of the males said that they did not know. The youth consultants associated with this study interpreted this to mean that "many teens were not motivated enough even to explore the availability of contraception in their area and that it was this lack of motivation and its underlying causes that result in nonuse of contraception by the majority of teens" (Ross, 1979: 39). The fact that service availability has this subjective component makes it difficult to assess whether race differences in access to services are a factor in the higher fertility of young blacks. Since few researchers have elected to study the supply of services, particularly the subjective aspects, the difficulty of assessing differences is heightened.

Another consideration is the contention that the availability of family planning services and abortion increase the incidence of adolescent pregnancy because they encourage early sexual activity and/or contraceptive carelessness (Roylance, 1981). According to this perspective, service availability cannot solve the problem of adolescent pregnancy, because the availability of services causes or at least exacerbates the problem. However, a number of studies indicate that greater availability of family planning services was associated with lower fertility in the early to mid-1970s among blacks and whites and that abortion availability was related to lower fertility, particularly among whites (Forrest, 1980; Moore and Caldwell, 1977; Borders and Cutright, 1979; Cutright and Jaffe, 1976). Thus we assume that a greater availability of services is related to lower fertility. One cannot assume, though, that the relationship is necessarily linear. At some point, the impact on fertility of increasing services begins to diminish. The point at which this would occur is not known, but we do not expect the effect to ever become negative—that is, more services are not expected to lead to more pregnancies. With these caveats, we posit that greater availability of services should lower fertility and that if services are more available to one group than another their fertility should be lower. We measure service availability by the number of clinics in operation and the number of patients served.

The Availability of Contraceptive Services to Teenagers

Family Planning Services

Subsidized family planning programs were initiated during the late 1960s, grew rapidly during the early 1970s, and then grew more slowly during the late 1970s. In 1968, an estimated 1,400 agencies provided organized family planning services to 863,000 patients. In 1980, 2,530 agencies served 4,644,000 patients (Alan Guttmacher Institute, 1982). During these years, the proportion of young patients and white patients has grown. In 1969, 20 percent of the patients served were under age 20, compared to 33 percent in 1980.

As more young patients have been served, more white patients have also been served. In 1969, 59 percent of clinic patients were black, compared to 26 percent in 1980. Thus clinics continue to serve disproportionate numbers of blacks, but this is less the case than it was a decade ago. This appears to have resulted from an expansion of services to low-income white women, so that the current racial distribution of patients has come to more closely approximate the racial distribution of low- and marginal-income women in the United States (Alan Guttmacher Institute, 1982).[1] As shown in Table 4.1, the proportion of low-income women served by organized family planning clinics has risen among both blacks and whites, but more so among whites, so that by 1980 approximately equal proportions of low-income whites and blacks were served by family planning clinics. (Many women are not served

TABLE 4.1
Family Planning Program Patients under 200 Percent of Poverty as Percentage of Women Ages 15–44 under 200 Percent of Poverty

Year	White	Nonwhite
CY1970	3.3	16.6
CY1975	19.7	32.4
CY1980	26.9	29.0

Source: Alan Guttmacher Institute, "Current Functioning and Future Priorities in Family Planning Services Delivery," December 1982, p. 35.

because they are not sexually active or fecund, because they are pregnant, or because they prefer to attend a private physician.)

The proportion of patients who have no children has also risen over the past decade, so that by 1980 a majority of patients were childless (see Table 4.2). The increased proportion of teenagers served is partially responsible for this trend, since the majority of teenage patients are childless, particularly among whites (see Table 4.3).

The fact that a higher proportion of black than white teenage clinic patients have already had a child represents an important race difference. Given the proportion of blacks who have sex at very young ages, it is difficult to provide services young enough. Only 7 percent of the black teens served by clinics in 1978 were 14 or younger (National Center for Health Statistics, 1981), yet 37 percent of sexually experienced black female teens report being 14 or younger at first intercourse (Zelnik and Shah, 1983). Among whites, about 2 percent of patients were 14 or younger, compared to 19 percent of the sexually experienced whose first sexual experience occurred when they were less than 15. (This gap is even larger than it would appear since the denominator includes only sexually experienced females, and fewer white teens have had premarital sex. Published data are weighted and this precludes calculation of the more relevant statistics.)

The higher proportion of blacks who are very young when they first have intercourse is associated with a higher incidence of unprotected intercourse. As shown in Table 4.4, younger teens, black and white, male and female, are less likely to use contraception when they first have sexual intercourse (see also Zabin and Clark, 1981). However, at any given age, blacks are less

TABLE 4.2
Family Planning Program Patients by Parity (patient numbers in thousands)

Number of Live Births	1969		1975		1980	
	N	%	N	%	N	%
0	99	9	1,909	49	2,522	54
1	496	46	866	22	1,026	22
2	--	--	553	14	627	14
3 or more	475	45	596	15	469	10
Total	1,070	100	3,924	100	4,644	100

Source: Alan Guttmacher Institute, "Current Functioning and Future Priorities in Family Planning Services Delivery," December 1982, p. 36.

TABLE 4.3
**Number and Percentage of Female Family Planning Patients under 20 and
Percentage Distribution by Pregnancy History by Race, 1978**

	Race		
	Total[a]	White	Black
All patients			
Number in thousands	1,268	892	355
Percentage	100.0	70.3	28.0
	Percent distribution		
Total	100.0	100.0	100.0
Number of pregnancies			
None	65.8	69.9	54.6
One	26.3	23.3	33.5
Two or more	8.1	6.7	11.5
Number of live births			
None	78.5	83.4	65.3
One	18.0	13.9	28.7
Two or more	3.5	2.7	5.9
Number of fetal deaths			
None	84.9	84.7	85.1
One	13.3	13.4	13.2
Two or more	2.0	1.9	0.2

[a]Includes races other than white and black.

Note: Numbers may not add to totals due to rounding.

Source: National Center for Health Statistics, "Teenagers Who Use Organized Family Planning
Services: United States, 1978," 1981, Table B.

likely to use a method. Blacks are more likely to use a prescription method
if they use a method; but they are less likely to use any method.

In other words, black females initiating intercourse are less likely to use
contraception both because contraceptive use is lower among blacks and also
because they are disproportionately young when they begin to have sex. As
one might expect, then, blacks are more likely to become pregnant within a
given number of months after they first have intercourse. This racial difference
is reduced when the probability of pregnancy is examined among groups of
young women who were about the same age when they first had sex (see

TABLE 4.4

Percentage of Women Ages 15–19 and Men Ages 17–21 Whose First Sexual Intercourse Involved the Use of a Contraceptive Method, and Percentage of Users Who Relied on a Prescription Method, by Age at First Intercourse, According to Race

Age at First Intercourse	Percentage Who Used Any Method			Percentage Who Used Prescription Method		
	Total	White	Black	Total	White	Black
Women	45.9	51.2	40.8	19.9	15.3	40.7
Under 15	31.0	33.2	26.9	10.2	4.7	22.9
15 - 17	52.1	52.9	48.8	18.8	12.1	48.0
18 or more	62.3	63.7	47.7	29.4	28.9	a
Men	44.1	46.0	34.0	22.0	21.6	25.1
Under 15	34.0	36.4	27.8	16.8	15.6	20.8
15 - 17	48.5	48.9	44.7	20.5	19.2	34.1
18 or more	59.1	59.4	a	38.3	40.0	a

[a]Fewer than 20 cases; in all others, N ≥ 30.

Source: M. Zelnik and F. Shah, ''First Intercourse among Young Americans,'' *Family Planning Perspectives* 15(1983).

Table 4.5). However, differences related to race are larger and more consistent than differences related to age, so age is not the only factor involved.

To explore this further, we have calculated the proportions of black teens and white teens provided with family planning services either by a family planning clinic or by a private physician (see Table 4.6). As a proportion of all teens, more blacks are served than are whites. This is to be expected, since a larger proportion of young blacks are sexually active (see chapter 2). Correcting our proportion to represent only those teens who have had sex or who are married, similar proportions of blacks and whites are served. A higher proportion of blacks are served by organized family planning clinics, while a higher proportion of whites are served by private physicians. Overall, though, about half of those estimated to be in need of services seem to receive services.[2] Of course, this implies that about half of those at risk of pregnancy are not receiving medical care. Some of these are pregnant or are seeking to become pregnant. Others are relying on nonprescription methods. Still others are not using any method.

National data from the 1979 Johns Hopkins survey indicate that black couples are considerably less likely to rely on male nonprescription methods

TABLE 4.5
Estimated Cumulative Percentage of Metropolitan-Area Women Ages 15–19 Who Have Ever Had a Premarital First Pregnancy, by Number of Months following First Intercourse, According to Race and Age at First Intercourse, 1979

| Months after First Intercourse | Age at First Intercourse | | | | Age at First Intercourse | | | |
| | Whites | | | | Blacks | | | |
	All Ages	< 15 (N=92)	15–16 (N=197)	> 17 (N=125)	All Ages	< 15 (N=153)	15–16 (N=176)	> 17 (N=72)
3	12.8	10.8	14.1	12.0	14.2	13.5	12.0	20.9
6	14.8	12.5	15.6	15.0	20.4	17.8	20.2	26.2
12	22.0	19.8	24.1	19.1	28.8	29.6	27.7	27.2
18	29.4	32.9	29.1	21.4	36.2	38.7	33.5	33.9
24	33.2	39.0	31.5	a	43.3	43.6	43.1	42.7

[a]N < 15.
Source: M. Koenig and M. Zelnik, "The Risk of Premarital First Pregnancy among Metropolitan-Area Teenagers: 1976 and 1979," Family Planning Perspectives 14(1982), Tables 1, 3.

of contraception at first intercourse and more likely to use no method (Zelnik and Shah, 1983). When they do use a method of contraception, blacks are more likely to use a female method, particularly the pill, while whites are considerably more likely to rely on a male method for their first method. Perhaps cost is a factor. Since clinic methods are often subsidized while drug store methods must be purchased, the greater affluence of white teens on average may mean nonprescription methods are more accessible to whites. Thus, Zelnik and Kantner (1980) report that the pill was the first method for 38 percent of black females and 15 percent of white females. However, about one-third of each race relied on condoms for their first method and 42 percent of whites compared to 13 percent of blacks relied first on withdrawal, a method which involves no expenditure. Perhaps cost affects the proportion not using any method. Overall, blacks were more likely to never use any method of contraception, a tendency which is strongly related to a higher probability of pregnancy (Table 4.7) (Zelnik and Kantner, 1980; Koenig and Zelnik, 1982). Thus blacks are both more likely than whites to have been protected by a prescription method and more likely to be unprotected at first intercourse.

Nonsupply Factors

It is important to note that a number of other factors also affect the probability of pregnancy and may differ by race. These include frequency of

TABLE 4.6
Estimates of Proportion of All Teens Served by Organized Family Planning Clinics and Private Physicians, Under Several Assumptions, by Race, 1980

		Whites (%)	Blacks (%)
Percentage of All Teens 15 to 19 Served by Clinics or Private Physicians[a]		27	35
Percentage of All Sexually Experienced and Married Teens Served by Clinics	AGI[a]	23	38
	NCHS[b]	25	42
Percentage of All Sexually Experienced and Married Teens Served by Private Physicians[a]		23	11
Percentage of All Sexually Experienced and Married Teens Served by Private Physicians	AGI[a]	46	49
	NCHS[b]	49	53

[a]Number of females under 20 served in organized family planning clinics and number served by private physicians are from the Alan Guttmacher Institute, "Current Functioning and Future Priorities in Family Planning Services Delivery," December 1982.
[b]Number of female family planning patients under age 20 in 1980 from National Health Survey, National Center for Health Statistics, "Basic Data on Women Who Use Family Planning Clinics: United States, 1980," Table 1.

Note: Among all women ages 15–44, 91 percent of the visits to private physicians in 1977 were made by whites: B. Cypress, "Family Planning Visits to Private Physicians," *Family Planning Perspectives* 11(July/August 1979): 234–36. The same proportion was assumed for teenagers. Percentages reported in Zelnik and Shah, "First Intercourse among Young Americans," *Family Planning Perspectives* 15(March/April 1983): 68, indicate the number using private physicians may be higher among both blacks and whites, but numbers are not provided. The number of teenage women in need of family planning services might be further reduced by taking out some number of teenage women estimated to be seeking pregnancy and thus not desiring contraception. Data on the proportion of teenagers who become premaritally pregnant reveal a small racial difference, with 21 percent of black teens and 16 percent of white teens having intended to become pregnant premaritally, and more black youth desire early pregnancy (see chapter 7). However, good data for estimating this proportion among teenagers by race do not exist. In addition, pregnancy testing is among the family planning services provided. Moreover, adjusting would deflate the black denominator more than the white; thus not deflating is more conservative. Therefore, this particular adjustment was not made.

Sources: Population and marital status data obtained from the U.S. Bureau of the Census. Data on premarital sexual activity for 1979 were used. They were obtained from M. Zelnik and J. Kantner, "Sexual Activity, Contraceptive Use and Pregnancy Among Metropolitan Area Teenagers: 1971–1979," *Family Planning Perspectives* 12(1980): 230–37. Married teenagers are assumed to be sexually active.

intercourse, regularity of contraceptive use, correct use of method, fecundity, and method failure. While not the focus of concern here, a brief overview seems warranted.

Although blacks tend to initiate sexual activity in higher proportions and at earlier ages, sexually experienced blacks appear to have intercourse slightly

TABLE 4.7

Estimated Cumulative Percent of Females Ages 15–19 with Premarital First Pregnancy, by Duration since First Intercourse, by Race and Contraceptive Use Status, 1979

Months After First Intercourse	All Premaritally Sexually Experienced Females			Teens Who Never Used Contraceptive Method			Teens Who Always Used Contraceptive Method		
	Total (%)	White (%)	Black (%)	Total (%)	White (%)	Black (%)	Total (%)	White (%)	Black (%)
3	13	14	14	20	21	18	4%	5%	2%
6	16	15	20	25	22	28	5	6	4
12	24	22	29	35	32	38	9	10	7
18	31	29	36	44	43	46	10	10	9
24	36	33	43	50	48	52	12	11	14

Source: M. Koenig and M. Zelnik, "The Risk of Premarital First Pregnancy among Metropolitan-Area Teenagers: 1976 and 1979," *Family Planning Perspectives* 14(1982): 239–47.

less frequently than whites (Zelnik et al., 1981; Zabin and Clark, 1981). Frequency of intercourse may lead to more regular contraceptive use if sex becomes predictable. As a measure of exposure to pregnancy, though, the lower frequency of blacks should lower the risk of pregnancy.

Though sex is less frequent among blacks, fecundity may be higher. Black females appear to be slightly more physiologically mature at each chronological age, net of parental education and socioeconomic status, relative to whites (Harlan et al., 1980). These differences are too small to account for the large differences in pregnancy probability among sexually experienced teens, though. Consistency and effectiveness of contraceptive use remain to be considered.

Blacks appear to be slightly less likely to use contraceptive methods regularly (see Table 4.8) and, among those becoming pregnant, blacks are more likely than whites to have had an unwanted pregnancy when not using a contraceptive (see Table 4.9). However, inconsistent use is high among whites as well as blacks. In addition, it seems likely that incorrect use is high among both blacks and whites, given the data that have been collected on understanding of the menstrual cycle and pregnancy risk (see Table 3.2).

Data on the proportion pregnant according to how consistently the teens used contraception (Table 2.14) indicate no racial difference among consistent users. Among never-users blacks are somewhat more likely to have become pregnant. Among inconsistent users, blacks are much more likely to have

TABLE 4.8

Percentage Distribution of Premaritally Sexually Experienced Females 15–19, by Whether Used Contraception[a] Prior to Interview/Marriage/Pregnancy, by Race, 1979

Contraceptive Use	Total	White	Black
Always used	34.2	35.0	31.2
Sometimes used	39.2	41.0	33.0
Never used	26.6	24.0	35.9
Percent who used contraception at first intercourse	48.9%	51.1%	40.9%

[a]Contraceptive methods include the pill, IUD, diaphragm, condom, foam, douche, withdrawal, and rhythm.

Source: M. Zelnik and J. Kantner, "Sexual Activity, Contraceptive Use and Pregnancy among Metropolitan-Area Teenagers: 1971–1979," Family Planning Perspectives 12(1980): 230–237.

TABLE 4.9
**Percentage Distributions of Women Ages 15–19 Who Ever Experienced a
Premarital First Pregnancy and Were Married at the Time the Pregnancy Was
Resolved, by Pregnancy Intention and, among Those Who Did Not Want the
Pregnancy, by Contraceptive Use According to Race, 1979[a]**

Pregnancy Intention and Contraceptive Use	1979		
	Total	White	Black
Pregnancy Intention	(N=312)	(N=115)	(N=197)
Wanted	18.0	16.4	20.9
Not wanted	82.0	83.6	79.1
Did Not Want Pregnancy	(N=246)	(N=94)	(N=152)
Used contraception	31.5	36.1	22.0
Did not use	68.5	63.9	78.0
Total	100.0	100.0	100.0

[a]Includes respondents pregnant at time of interview.

Source: M. Zelnik and J. Kantner, "Sexual Activity, Contraceptive Use and Pregnancy among
     Metropolitan-Area Teenagers: 1971–1979," *Family Planning Perspectives* 12(1980),
     Table 6.

become pregnant. Unfortunately, analyses of inconsistent users from the National Survey of Young Women have not been published and research on factors leading to inconsistent use among teens is only beginning to accumulate. Since the probability of pregnancy does differ by race when all teenagers are considered and since inconsistent users comprise about a third of all sexually active teens (see Table 4.8), it appears that racial differences in the regularity or correctness of use must exist. However, exactly what these differences are and the factors leading to inconsistent use must await further research.

While the difference in the overall proportion of sexually experienced teens becoming pregnant within two years is substantial—43 percent among blacks versus 33 percent among whites—it is important to keep in mind that this is only part of the picture. Black females are also more likely to have had sex. In fact, larger racial differences exist in the proportion of females of a given age who are sexually experienced (see Table 2.11). Thus, a larger fraction of black teens are exposed to the risk of premarital pregnancy and, among those having premarital sex, the odds of pregnancy are somewhat higher among blacks.

Contraception: Discussion

Several conclusions appear warranted. Teenage blacks are more likely to be at risk of pregnancy than whites because they more often initiate sex as teenagers. They also begin to have intercourse at younger ages and younger teens are less likely to contracept. In addition, blacks are at greater risk because they are less likely to ever use a method of contraception; 36 percent of black teen females had never used a method compared to 24 percent of whites. When initiating sex, blacks are less likely to use male methods, particularly withdrawal, which provide at least some protection relative to using no method. On the other hand, blacks are not placed at greater risk because they are less likely than whites to avail themselves of family planning services. About half of blacks and whites obtain family planning services from a medical source, blacks more from clinics and whites more from private physicians. Whites may be better able to afford private physician care, while blacks in low-income urban areas may have better access to clinics, which are often located in urban areas and charge fees based on a sliding income scale. In addition, inconsistent use is high among both blacks and whites and, among young women who come to family planning clinics, blacks do not seem to delay their first visit longer than whites. An average of a year or more seems typical, though delays are much greater when intercourse is initiated very young (Zabin and Clark, 1981). However, among young women who are inconsistent in their use of a method, blacks are more likely to become pregnant, a difference for which there is no ready explanation and which merits further investigation.

Data indicate that blacks are less likely to use any method prior to pregnancy. Other data, though, indicate that blacks are more likely to use the pill as their first method of birth control. This suggests a willingness to use clinic methods. At the same time it seems that black couples need to be urged to use birth control more immediately after initiating sex, if not before. However, this need is very great among young white couples as well. It seems most appropriate to conclude that teenagers, both black and white, need to receive family planning services earlier than they do. This requires, of course, increasing the demand for family planning services among sexually active teens.

This is not to say that the availability and accessibility of family planning methods—the supply of services—is of no concern. In fact, the supply of services is a very important concern for both blacks and for whites. Researchers have found that a number of factors predict greater clinic attendance among teens, including special outreach and follow-up activities, provision of free services to teens, and seeing young clients without a formal appointment (Chamie et al., 1982); having insight into the cultural beliefs and practices of patients (Poland and Beane, 1980); having clinic hours that are convenient for students (Philliber and Namerow, 1983); having a diversity of locations and provider types (Dryfoos and Heisler, 1978); recognizing teenagers' concern that their parents will be told of their visit (Zabin and Clark, 1981); making it easier and less embarrassing for males to obtain male methods (Meara, 1981; Ross, 1979); and having a staff that expresses warmth and caring and has rapport with young people (Philliber and Jones, 1982). Developing service programs that address these kinds of special needs and concerns among teenagers seems likely to increase service accessibility for both blacks and whites. In addition, some research suggests that black and white teens have some priorities that differ. Zabin and Clark (1981) report that confidentiality and the fact that their friends attend a particular clinic are particularly important to white teens. The proximity of the clinic to their home and the staff's concern for teenagers were ranked highest by black teens attending a clinic. In addition, blacks teens were found more likely to be attending a clinic because their mother chose it for them.

Further research exploring ways to make services more available and accessible is needed. In addition, research evaluating ways to encourage teenagers to seek services, including both methods and instruction, as soon as they decide to initiate sex would be very useful. The age, race, and sex of teenagers at risk should all be considered as programs are developed to reach sexually active teens or teens expecting to become active as early as possible. The acceptability of available services may be as great a concern as the absolute availability of services. Factors affecting teenagers' perception of the availability and accessibility of services may differ by race, but the basic conclusion must be that services need to be more widely accessible to all teenagers. In addition, ways must be found to encourage teenagers to use those services that are available sooner and more efficiently.

At present, the high rate of unintended pregnancy among teens results not only in a high rate of unintended teenage motherhood but also in a high reliance on abortion among teenagers.

Abortion

A discussion of services for teenagers cannot ignore the importance of abortion. Teenagers obtain more than 450,000 abortions annually in the United States, and the birth rate among teenagers would be substantially higher if teenagers did not resort to abortion in such large numbers.

The younger the pregnant teenager, the more likely she is to obtain an abortion. Among young women less than 15 in 1980, 10,169 births occurred compared to 15,340 abortions. Among women 15 to 17, 198,222 births took place compared to 183,350 abortions. Among women aged 18 to 19, there were 353,939 births and 261,430 abortions (National Center for Health Statistics, 1982; Henshaw and O'Reilly, 1983).

Overall, blacks are disproportionately likely to resort to abortion (see Table 4.10). Black women obtained nearly 30 percent of all abortions in 1980 and they had an abortion rate more than double that of white women, 56.8 abortions per 1,000 women compared to 24.3 among whites. Black women terminated an estimated 39.2 percent of their pregnancies in abortion, compared to 27.4 percent among white women. Though abortion is widely used worldwide, in our view this level of reliance on abortion in a modern industrial nation is appalling.

Abortion rates are highest among women in their twenties among both blacks and whites, followed by women in their teens (see Table 4.11). Since most abortions are obtained by unmarried and childless women, this pattern is not surprising. At every age, though, abortion rates are higher among black women (see Table 4.12). Black and white rates are most similar during the years 15 to 19; but even then the black rate is 1.7 times as high as the white rate. (Considering all females 12 to 19, this ratio seems to have risen over the 1970s and then fallen recently as white rates continued to climb while the black rate has risen only slightly; see Table 4.13.) In addition, black women are more likely to obtain abortions than whites even when they are married. Among whites, married women obtain abortions at a rate of 9 per

TABLE 4.10

Number and Percentage Distribution of Abortions, Abortion Rate per 1,000 Women Ages 15–44, and Percentage of Pregnancies Terminated by Abortion, by Race, Selected Years

	1974	1977	1978	1979	1980
Number of Abortions	898,570	1,316,700	1,409,600	1,497,670	1,553,890
White	629,320	888,780	969,410	1,062,400	1,093,630
Nonwhite	269,250	427,920	440,190	435,270	460,260
Percentage Distribution of Abortions					
White	70.0	67.5	68.8	70.9	70.4
Nonwhite	30.0	32.5	31.2	29.1	29.6
Total	100.0	100.0	100.0	100.0	100.0
Abortion Rate					
White	15.7	20.9	22.3	24.0	24.3
Nonwhite	41.4	59.0	58.7	56.2	56.8
Percentage of Pregnancies Terminated by Abortion					
White	19.6	25.0	26.1	27.1	27.4
Nonwhite	31.6	40.4	39.6	38.2	39.2

Source: Stanley Henshaw and Kevin O'Reilly, "Characteristics of Abortion Patients in the United States, 1979 and 1980," *Family Planning Perspectives* 15(1983): 5–16.

TABLE 4.11
Number of Legal Abortions and Abortion Rate per 1,000 Women by Age of Woman, 1974, 1977, and 1980

	1974	1977	1980
Abortion Rate--Total	19.3	26.4	29.3
Under 15	6.4	7.6	8.4
15 - 19	26.9	37.5	42.9
15 - 17	u	(26.2)	(30.2)
18 - 19	u	(54.1)	(61.0)
20 - 24	30.4	44.3	51.4
25 - 29	19.6	26.9	30.8
30 - 34	13.0	15.7	17.1
35 - 39	8.4	9.8	9.3
40 or over	3.3	3.9	3.5
Number of Abortions--Total	898,570	1,316,700	1,553,890
Under 15	13,420	15,650	15,340
15 - 19	278,280	396,630	444,780
15 - 17	u	(165,610)	(183,350)
18 - 19	u	(231,020)	(261,430)
20 - 24	286,600	449,660	549,410
25 - 29	162,690	246,680	303,820
30 - 34	89,810	124,380	153,060
35 - 39	48,770	61,700	66,580
40 or over	19,000	22,000	20,900

u = unavailable.

Source: Stanley Henshaw and Kevin O'Reilly, "Characteristics of Abortion Patients in the United States, 1979 and 1980," *Family Planning Perspectives* 15(1983): 5–16.

1,000 women, compared to a rate of 44 per 1,000 among unmarried women. Among blacks, the rate is 34 per 1,000 married women and 68 per 1,000 unmarried women. Obviously, unwanted pregnancy is a problem for many black women who are older and married, as well as unmarried teens.

Calculations prepared by Henshaw and O'Reilly (1983) indicate little difference in the rate of pregnancy by race when intended pregnancies are considered (see Table 4.14). However, black women are substantially more likely to experience unintended pregnancies and even their higher abortion rate is insufficient to erase the difference in their birth rate due to their much higher incidence of unwanted pregnancy.

Since abortion became legal nationwide in 1973, the frequency of abortion among black teenagers has risen greatly. In part this appears to represent the substitution of legal for illegal abortion, but the level of increase indicates that an absolute increase in the incidence of abortion has also occurred. In 1972, black teenagers had an estimated abortion rate of 17.4 per 1,000 young

TABLE 4.12
Abortions per 1,000 Women by Age and Race, and Ratio of White Rate to
Nonwhite Rate, 1980

| | Abortion Rate | | Nonwhite/ |
	White	Nonwhite	White Ratio
Under 15	5.0	24.4	4.9
15 - 19	38.3	66.0	1.7
20 - 24	43.1	95.6	2.2
25 - 29	24.5	64.7	2.6
30 - 34	13.3	38.9	2.9
35 - 39	7.4	21.0	2.8
40 or over	3.0	6.7	2.2

Source: Stanley Henshaw and K. O'Reilly, ''Characteristics of U.S. Abortion Patients in the United States, 1979 and 1980,'' *Family Planning Perspectives* 15(1983): 5–16.

women (see Table 4.14). By 1978, the rate had risen to 51.2. The rate rose among white teenagers as well, but it was twice as high among black as among white teens in 1978 reflecting the higher pregnancy rate of black teens. The ratio of abortions to live births also rose steeply for both black and white teens over the 1970s, but the black ratio rose particularly rapidly. In 1972, the abortion ratio was lower among black teens than white, but by 1978 it was higher among black teens. This increase is believed to have resulted from the increased availability of abortion following the 1973 Supreme Court decision (Ezzard et al., 1982).

Despite their disproportionate reliance on abortion, black teenage women are estimated to have a greater unmet need for abortion than are white teenagers (Alan Guttmacher Institute, 1981, Figure 56). In 1978, a total of 419,000 young women 15 to 19 were estimated to receive abortions and another 160,000 were estimated to require them but not obtain an abortion. Among whites, it is estimated that 309,000 teenagers obtained abortions, and 78,000 wanted an abortion but did not obtain one. Among blacks, it is estimated that 110,000 teenage women obtained abortions while another 72,000 wanted but did not obtain one.

The availability of abortion may have declined slightly since 1978 due to the restriction on federal funding of abortion. Because blacks are more likely to be eligible for Medicaid, the funding restriction may have disproportionately reduced the incidence of abortion among blacks (Henshaw and O'Reilly, 1983). Nevertheless, since the total number of abortions obtained by blacks

TABLE 4.13

Estimated Abortion Rate per 1,000 Women Ages 12–19,[a] and Ratio of Abortions per 1,000 Live Births to Women Ages 12 to 19, by Race

Year	Abortion Rate Per 1,000 Women White	Black[b]	Ratio of White to Black Rate	Abortion Ratio Per 1,000 Live Births White	Black[b]
1972	11.7	17.4	1.5	270	186
1973	14.1	25.4	1.8	338	283
1974	16.0	34.0	2.1	388	395
1975	18.0	42.0	2.3	449	503
1976	19.8	48.1	2.4	509	602
1977	22.2	50.7	2.3	558	627
1978	24.3	51.2	2.1	615	643

[a]Based on age at conception.
[b]Including teenagers of all other racial minorities.
Source: N.V. Ezzard, W. Cates, Jr., D.G. Kramer, and C. Tietze, "Race-Specific Patterns of Abortion Use by American Teenagers," *American Journal of Public Health* 72(1982): 809.

TABLE 4.14

Pregnancy Rate per 1,000 Women Ages 15–44, by Pregnancy Intention at Time of Conception and Pregnancy Outcome, and Percentage of Unintended Pregnancies Terminated by Abortion, According to Race, 1976

Pregnancy Intention and Outcome	Total	White	Nonwhite
Pregnancy Rate	104	95	165
Intended Pregnancies	48	49	46
Live births	40	41	38
Spontaneous fetal loss	8	8	8
Unintended Pregnancies	56	46	119
Live births	25	21	48
Abortions	24	19	56
Spontaneous fetal loss	7	6	15
Percentage of Unwanted Pregnancies Terminated by Abortion	43	41	47

Note: Spontaneous fetal loss includes estimated miscarriages and stillbirths.
Source: S. Henshaw and K. O'Reilly, "Characteristics of Abortion Patients in the United States, 1979 and 1980," *Family Planning Perspectives* 15(1983): 5–16.

has not fallen, the effect cannot be large. A study by Trussell et al. (1980) also suggests that the magnitude of the effect of the Medicaid cutoff has been modest.

Evidence that there is a substantial unmet need for abortion and that blacks are disproportionately in need of more available services suggests that abortion services should be more available. Recommendations to increase the availability and accessibility of abortion are readily available. Restoring federal coverage of abortion under Medicaid and other programs, increasing the number of providers, establishing providers in counties without services, and providing abortions without parental consent or notification seem likely to increase reliance on abortion (Henshaw et al., 1981; Alan Guttmacher Institute, 1981; Henshaw and O'Reilly, 1983). We cannot give high priority to these recommendations, however, given the fact that abortion is already so highly relied on by teenagers and minority women. Higher priority should be given, in our view, to efforts to reduce the incidence of early pregnancy.

Conclusions

We estimate that about half of all sexually active teenagers are receiving family planning services. Whites are more likely to be served by private physicians while blacks are more likely to be served in family planning clinics; however, the proportion of those receiving services does not vary greatly by race. Another way to say this would be that the levels of unmet need appear to be very high among teens, both black and white.

It has been our goal to assess whether services are equally available to blacks and whites, to see whether such a difference could account for the considerably higher birth rate among black teens. Since the proportion of black and white teens at risk of pregnancy who receive medical family planning services is approximately equal, the supply of services does not seem to be the factor. Both blacks and whites are in need of family planning services. Yet "supply" is a very subjective and slippery concept where contraception is concerned. If more teenagers seek services, the supply will expand. The accessibility of available services seems to be an issue as great or greater than simple supply. How can barriers due to location, cost, staff characteristics, hours of operation, waiting time, etc. be lowered to make services more accessible?

Demand for services seems to be even more crucial. Examples abound of efforts to increase enrollment and encourage patients to make return visits to clinics (e.g., Namerow et al., 1983). It can be very difficult to get teens to use available services. How can teens be made to perceive that if they are having sex they need to take some action to prevent early pregnancy? How can demand be increased?

In the course of our review, some relevant racial differences were noted. One such difference is the age at which teens initiate intercourse. The earlier initiation of sex among black teens is a factor in black teens' higher pregnancy rates, since contraception is less likely among those younger when they have first intercourse. The difference may also be related to less consistent use of contraception among blacks. In addition, a higher proportion of black teens never use birth control prior to pregnancy and, not surprisingly, this is associated with a considerably higher probability of pregnancy.

Given their higher pregnancy rate, black teenagers are also disproportionately likely to resort to abortion. Black teens have an abortion rate approximately double that of white teenagers. Because of the higher incidence of pregnancy among black teens, even this higher reliance on abortion does not eradicate the difference in teenage birth rates by race. One might then conclude that greater availability of abortion is needed; however, in view of the extremely high reliance on abortion occurring at present we place higher priority on the prevention of unintended pregnancy.

Prevention would be facilitated by a delay in the onset of sexual activity, since older teenagers seem better able to be diligent contraceptors. Given the earlier initiation of sexual activity among blacks, this recommendation could have a particularly large impact among blacks. Among teenagers who are sexually active or who expect to be, earlier and more consistent use of contraception is urgently needed among both blacks and whites and particularly among blacks. Since "just didn't get around to it" is the most frequently cited reason given by teens for delaying their first visit to a contraceptive clinic (Zabin and Clark, 1981), it is important to consider in some depth the motivations, or the lack thereof, that lead teenagers to have sexual intercourse without using contraception.

Notes

1. It seems possible, though, that a contraction in the number of women served may be occurring as a result of recent reductions in funding for family planning services. From a high of $377 million in FY1981, total federal and state appropriations fell to an estimated $333 million in FY1982 (U.S. House of Representatives, Select Committee on Children, Youth, and Families, 1983). If the supply of services falls, conclusions based on current data may become inappropriate.
2. A recent estimate for 1981 suggests that 57 percent of teenagers at risk received medical family planning services. Separate figures by race were not estimated. See A. Torres and J.D. Forrest, "Family Planning Clinic Services in the United States, 1981," *Family Planning Perspectives* 15(1983): 272–78.

5

Education as a Motivating Factor

School enrollment and motherhood are both demanding activities and are difficult to combine. Many young mothers find it impossible to continue with their schooling. We expect the reverse to hold as well—youths who wish to continue their education tend to postpone parenthood. Therefore, teenagers' educational and occupational aspirations are hypothesized to affect their fertility behavior. Specifically, if a teenager has high aspirations she may be more motivated to postpone having sex, or if she engages in sex she may be more likely to take precautions to prevent pregnancy. This motivation may be tempered if the individual has low expectations that she will be able to achieve her goals or faces high barriers to fulfilling her goals. If this hypothesis holds, then it could explain some of the differences between blacks and whites since there are differences in the array of opportunities available to young black and white women. A brief statement of the hypothesis is as follows:

1. A young woman's decisions with regard to sex and birth control are affected by her educational aspirations and expectations and that:
   - A girl with high ambition and high opportunity will be highly motivated to postpone sex and/or avoid pregnancy
   - A girl with high ambition and low opportunity or low ambition but high opportunity may not be as highly motivated
   - A girl with low ambition and low opportunity will have little or no incentive to postpone sex or pregnancy.

2. These combinations of ambition and opportunity differ by race, with blacks (and other minorities) having lower ambition or opportunity.
3. These differences in ambition and opportunity are at least partially responsible for black/white differences in fertility.

Education and Fertility

Several types of evidence exist that would tend to support the general idea that women with higher educational plans are less likely to have a birth. These include:

67

1. Data and research pertaining to older women documenting a strong association between higher education and both lower fertility rates and delayed childbearing.
2. Studies indicating that young women with lower aspirations and expectations are the most likely to have a child at a young age.

None of this evidence provides conclusive proof, however, that educational plans explain black-white fertility differences. Further evidence that aspirations or expectations are lower among blacks, or that low motivation is more strongly predictive of adolescent childbearing among blacks, or that blacks are very overrepresented among groups that tend to have low aspirations, is needed. In the next several sections we will review the several types of evidence that bear on this issue.

Educational Attainment and Fertility

A long-standing association between higher levels of education and small families has been documented (Westoff and Ryder, 1977). As shown in Table 5.1 for 1981, the number of births women have had is strongly related to the amount of schooling they have achieved. In addition, the number of births women expect to have and the proportion who anticipate being childless is also strongly related to women's educational attainment. This relationship holds among white, black, and Spanish-origin women. Racial and ethnic differences are apparent within educational categories; however, within each racial or ethnic group rising education is associated with declining fertility. Educational attainment appears to be both a cause and an effect of fertility. Thus, although early childbearing has been found to reduce schooling among teenage mothers (Hofferth and Moore, 1979; Card and Wise, 1978), educational attainment and educational goals have also been found to predict timing of the first birth both in studies of early childbearing (Card, 1977; Moore et al., 1978; Haggstrom et al., 1981) and in studies of delayed childbearing (Bloom and Trussell, 1983; Rindfuss et al., 1983; Rindfuss et al., 1980). In fact, a number of researchers have noted that substantial proportions of the adolescent mothers in their samples—one-third to one-half of the school-age mothers—had dropped out of school at least a year before having their first child (Moore et al., 1978; Koo and Bilsborrow, 1979; Rindfuss et al., 1980), creating a sample in which the direction of causality can only be from education to early childbearing.

Educational Plans and Teenage Fertility

Sexual Activity. A number of studies have been reported in which some aspect of the fertility process has been linked with educational aspirations or expectations. For example, in a reanalysis of the 1971 national survey of

TABLE 5.1
Births to Date and Lifetime Births Expected per 1,000 Women and Percentage of Women Who Expect to Have No Births, by Years of School Completed, 1981, Women Ages 18–34, by Race and Ethnicity

	Births to Date	Lifetime Births Expected	Percentage Expecting No Births
All races, 18 - 34	1,136	2,048	10.9
Less than 12 years	1,774	2,399	6.9
12 years	1,191	2,018	10.0
1 to 3 years college	840	1,996	11.9
4 years college	655	1,839	16.5
5 years college or more	614	1,697	19.5
Whites, 18 - 34	1,073	2,024	11.2
Less than 12 years	1,670	2,334	6.5
12 years	1,139	1,998	10.4
1 to 3 years college	803	1,995	12.1
4 years college	643	1,870	16.4
5 years college or more	604	1,679	20.2
Blacks, 18 - 34	1,576	2,207	9.0
Less than 12 years	2,197	2,666	7.5
12 years	1,553	2,136	7.2
1 year college or more	1,002	1,870	13.3
Spanish origin, 18 - 34[a]	1,479	2,343	7.1
Less than 12 years	2,000	2,694	4.4
12 years	1,279	2,201	8.3
1 year college or more	790	1,894	10.3

[a]Persons of Spanish origin may be of any race.

Note: Women responding uncertain are omitted.

Source: U.S. Bureau of the Census, *Fertility of American Women: June 1981,"* 1983, Current Population Reports, Series P-20, No. 378, Table 4.

young women, Devaney and Hubley (1981) report that both black and white teens with higher educational expectations were significantly less likely to initiate sexual activity, net of numerous other variables. Ladner (1971) found that young black women who wanted to continue with schooling past high school tended to postpone coitus due to fear that a pregnancy would undercut the possibility that they could fulfill their goals. Hogan and Kitagawa (1983) report that black teenagers in Chicago were 53 percent less likely to have had sex, net of numerous control variables, if they desired a college degree than if they did not. Miller and Simon (1980) also found that females with higher educational aspirations, especially those desiring college degrees, are older at the initiation of sexual intercourse. Similarly, in a decade-long prospective study of a sample of middle-class white teenagers, Jessor and Jessor (1975) and Jessor et al. (1983) find strong evidence that youth who place lower value on academic achievement and who have lower expectations for academic achievement are more likely to initiate sexual activity at a young age.

Pregnancy. The studies by Devaney and Hubley (1981) and by Hogan and Kitagawa (1983) also explored the effect of aspirations on the probability of pregnancy within multivariate models. Devaney and Hubley report that educational aspirations affect the probability of pregnancy among both blacks and whites, even after controlling for a number of measures of family background, age at first intercourse, and whether the teen always used contraception. Hogan and Kitagawa report that black teens lacking college aspirations are 85 percent more likely to become pregnant, net of family background and neighborhood characteristics. They note that girls with college aspirations are more likely to be efficient contraceptors.

Pregnancy Outcome. Educational aspirations have also been found related to pregnancy outcome among those teenagers who do become pregnant. Devaney and Hubley (1981) found that teens with higher aspirations were less likely to have a live birth, while Rickels (1983) found that the urban black teens in his sample who delivered were less often in school and less often expected further education after high school. Liebowitz et al. (1980) found that the young pregnant women in their California sample who had higher grade point averages were more likely to resolve their pregnancies in abortion.

Whether a Teen Has a Child. Studies looking at just whether or not a young woman has had a child have produced more mixed results. Howell and Frese (1982a,b) report that the educational aspirations a respondent had when interviewed in 1969, during late elementary school, had no effect on whether he or she had had a child by the reinterview date in 1975. Their sample was comprised of low-income Southern students. In an analysis of a similar longitudinal survey of students, the Southern Youth Study, White (1979) found white lower-class females with social mobility aspirations via education were more likely to delay the first birth. Using a rural subsample of the same data set, Marshall and Cosby (1977) found educational aspirations to be negatively related to both early marriage and early fertility. McLaughlin (1981), on the other hand, in a careful study employing the National Longitudinal Survey of Young Women, found no effect of educational aspirations on the probability of a birth. His variables were very carefully circumscribed though, so that aspirations reflected the desire for any education beyond the respondent's current education plus one year and a birth was counted only if it occurred more than 9 but less than 21 months after the reference time. Results from several studies cited above indicate that an effect on fertility is related to having quite high aspirations, such as desiring to complete college, so McLaughlin's very cautious measure may not be picking up a relationship that would have been noted using a more demanding measure of educational aspirations. Moore and Hofferth (1980) using the same data set found that being enrolled in a college preparatory curriculum was significantly and negatively related to age at first childbirth and that the effect was somewhat stronger for blacks than for whites.

Interviews conducted with black high school students as a part of the current project provide additional qualitiative validation for the hypothesis that educational aspirations and opportunities affect fertility behavior.

Interviews: "It Depends on Your Priorities"

In all of our interviews it was quite clear that the teenagers felt that educational ambitions would affect behavior—both with respect to engaging in sex and with respect to contraception. Students were asked to finish four stories about four young people with very different levels of ambition and opportunity. For all of the story stems in which college was presented as something desired by the boy or girl in the story or as an available opportunity, the teenagers interviewed weighed that factor when they projected the teenagers' decisions on sex and contraception. The effect was most pronounced for the individual who had both high ambition and high opportunity. In contrast, in the story stem where the girl was already behind in school and going with someone who did not like school, there was a consensus that there was no reason to postpone sex and either insufficient knowledge or little motivation to contracept.

Mary: High Ambition/High Opportunity

> Story Stem: Mary's father is a lawyer. Her parents have a comfortable home and can afford to give her most of the things she wants. She is 15 and is a good student who works hard. She would like to go to medical school. Lately she's been dating John and they really like each other. He also plans to go to college, and is saving money to help pay the way.

> What do you think will happen to the relationship between Mary and John over the next year or so? What will Mary and John be doing when they're 20? [Male groups were read the same story, but it was about John and his girlfriend Mary.]

In every interview, the future for Mary was clear. She comes from a family that can provide the resources for higher education and her ambition to go to college will prevail. A substantial proportion of the girls thought that Mary probably would not have sex because of her ambitions. Virtually everyone agreed that if she did have sex she would definitely use birth control because of her plans for the future. This even came through in one of the interviews with the males, in which John was the focus of the story and less information was provided on Mary's family and her ambition. One male, in response to a comment that Mary would get pregnant, said "I don't feel that way because of the main fact that she's saving her money up . . . [she] wants to make something out of her life."

The girls were practically unanimous in their opinion that the key to Mary's behavior was her desire to go to college and her knowledge that having a baby would reduce or eliminate her chances of achieving that goal. Typical comments were:

> She's a hard worker so I doubt if a pregnancy occurs.
>
> They won't stay together because of their futures.
>
> They don't want to get serious.
>
> They [are] both determined . . . to further themselves.

Betty: Low Ambition/Low Opportunity

> Story Stem: Betty is 15, but she is 2 years behind in school. She is thinking of dropping out. Her family isn't too well off and can't do much to help her. There aren't very many jobs in the area where she lives, and her older sister is unemployed. She is going with Michael who doesn't like school very well either. They really like each other.
>
> What do you think will happen to the relationship between Betty and Michael over the next year or so? What will Michael and Betty be doing when they're 20? [Males were presented the same story but it focused on Michael and his girlfriend Betty.]

It was universally accepted that Betty, who was already two years behind in school, had very little to look forward to. Consequently, there was no incentive to postpone a pregnancy. Many also felt that her low educational achievement indicated that she would not know about contraception or how to obtain it. Again the key factor was educational opportunity and ambition. As one person put it: "If [she's] two years [behind in school there is], . . . no hope for her, she ain't never going to be nothing." And because both Betty and her boyfriend are not doing well in school the interviewees felt they would have sex "since they don't have nothing going for them." Another said, "They don't care enough to talk about birth control."

Sandra: High Ambition/Low Opportunity.

> Story Stem: Sandra is the third of five kids. She is 15. Sandra's father left home when she was little. Her mother had a real hard time providing food and clothes for the family. She wants to be the first one in the family to finish college. She doesn't know how she can afford to go to college, though, and several months ago she started going out with a guy named Joe, and they really like one another.
>
> What do you think will happen to the relationship between Sandra and Joe over the next year or two? What do you think Sandra and Joe will be doing when they're 20? [Again, males were given this story about Joe and his girlfriend Sandra.]

The outcome for Sandra, who wanted to go to college but comes from a female-headed family in which no one had finished college, is not as clear as the first two cases. The teenagers were torn between the fact that Sandra was working toward college and the fear that she would be defeated by her environment and end up "just like her mother." But in every case where the interviewees felt that Sandra would avoid sex or pregnancy, they said it was her educational plans that would affect her behavior: "She's determined to do something, to go to college." and "College will be her priority. She wouldn't want to do anything to mess that up."

There is also the indication that "book learning" translates into knowledge about birth control. One girl said: "If she's smart enough to go to college, she's smart enough to use birth control. If she has big plans, she'll use birth control."

Karen: Low Ambition/High Opportunity.

> Story Stem: Karen is a very bright 15-year-old, but she has never gotten very good grades. No one in her family has finished high school, and they have a hard time getting by. One of the school counselors talked with her and said she could probably get a college scholarship if she got her grades up. She went to talk about things with her boyfriend Bill. They've been going together for almost a year, and they really like each other.
>
> What do you think will happen to the relationship between Karen and Bill over the next few years? What will Karen and Bill be doing when they're 20? [As before, males responded to a story about Bill and his girlfriend Karen.]

The outcome for Karen, who had not worked hard in school but who might be able to get a college scholarship, was also uncertain in the teenagers' minds. While the possibility of a college scholarship might influence her behavior, the students felt that her low grades indicated that she might not want to work hard enough to go to college. Some said she would not go to college because her grades were not good and no one in her family had finished college. Others said she would concentrate on her education (rather than her boy friend and, by implication, sex) if "she wants to finish college more than she wants married life." But both groups felt that Karen might not be sufficiently motivated to avoid a pregnancy. As one put it, "She's not doing well in school so maybe a side of her says she doesn't care."

Racial Differences in Educational Aspirations

Given the association between high educational attainment and lower fertility or delayed childbearing among adult women and given evidence both from previous studies and our interviews of a relationship between low educational aspirations and early childbearing, the questions we then addressed were:

- are there racial differences in these aspirations and expectations?
- are there racial differences in educational attainment?
- are these differences, if any, due to family background characteristics?
- are these differences large enough to explain a significant proportion of the racial difference in teenage childbearing?

Racial Differences in Educational Attainment, Aspirations, and Expectations

There are two types of information available on education. One set of studies focuses on educational attainment, the amount of education individuals with certain characteristics actually obtain. The other set focuses on educational aspirations and expectations. A few studies examine both aspirations and attainment; however, no studies simultaneously consider aspirations, fertility and attainment separately by race.

Attainment. The most definitive information available is on high school dropouts, their characteristics, and the factors that relate to dropping out. There are clear racial differences in the dropout rates that show up in national statistics and in longitudinal studies of young women. Both the National Longitudinal Survey of Young Women, which includes women who were ages 14 to 24 in 1968, and the more recent National Longitudinal Survey of Young Americans, which includes young people aged 14 to 21 in 1979, indicate that there are racial differences in dropping out of high school and in some of the factors related to dropping out.

In a study of the 1968 cohort of young women, Roderick and others (1974) found a dropout rate of 4 percent for whites and 11 percent for blacks between 1968 and 1969. Their analysis indicated that the intercolor differences were due to differences in socioeconomic background and to the age-grade lag. Dropping out was positively related to having a father who was not a high school graduate and to having attended high school in the South, both of which are more likely for blacks than for whites. The researchers also found that dropping out was more likely among those with low educational aspirations. Of those aspiring to four or more years of college, only one percent of whites and four percent of blacks dropped out. By contrast, among those with lower educational aspirations, 6 percent of whites and 17 percent of blacks dropped out. There was also a correlation between the lowering of educational aspirations and family income. In other words, a larger percentage of lower income than upper income girls reduced the level of education they aspired to between survey years.

In a later study using six years of data from the same sample Mott and Shaw (1978) examined the experiences of high school dropouts in comparison with their peers who completed high school but did not go on to college. They found that 55 percent of the white dropouts and 62 percent of the black dropouts gave marriage or pregnancy as the primary reason for dropping out. However, the distribution between marriage and pregnancy differs substantially. Among the whites who dropped out 6.9 percent gave pregnancy as the reason while 46.7 percent of the blacks did. In contrast, 48.1 percent of the whites but only 15.3 percent of the blacks gave marriage as their reason for leaving school. However, the authors admit that it is hard to distinguish between those who had their educational plans altered by an untimely pregnancy and those who accelerated marriage and childbearing as an alternative to an unhappy school situation.

In another study, Shaw (1982) examined the relationship between being in a single-parent family and dropping out for young women. This study matched mothers and daughters from two NLS cohorts (Young Women and Mature Women). She found that for whites, living in a single-parent household had no effect on school completion except through its effect on income. For black women, however, both low income and living in a single-parent home independently contributed to dropping out. Women from single-parent homes were also more likely to begin childbearing at a young age. Since the blacks were more likely to live in one-parent families (40 percent versus 16 percent) and lived in them for longer periods of time, this could explain part of the racial difference in dropout rates.

It is possible to infer some direction of causality from other information in the NLS studies but not all of the evidence leans in the same direction. Some of the evidence would suggest that whites were *more* likely to get pregnant after giving up on school. For example, only 33 percent of the black dropouts but 68 percent of white dropouts were *not* enrolled nine months before their first birth. Moreover, 21.4 percent of white dropouts but only 9.3 percent of black dropouts indicated a dislike of school as the primary reason for leaving school. And a substantial proportion of the black dropouts

(20 percent), but a much smaller percentage of the white dropouts (6 percent) had children before they left school. In addition, more of the black dropouts complete subsequent nonschool training. All of these might suggest that among black women it is childbearing that affects education while among whites it is low educational aspirations that precede childbearing.

In studies using the 1979 NLS, Rumberger (1981, 1982) found many of the same patterns and correlations that were found for the 1968 cohort. Blacks were three times as likely to be two or more years behind in school as whites (10 percent versus 3 percent), a major factor in dropping out. Among black females who dropped out, 41 percent cited pregnancy as the reason, compared to 17 percent for whites. Only 18 percent of black females compared to 27 percent of white females gave a dislike of school as the primary reason for leaving school.

Rumberger found that family background was a powerful predictor of dropout behavior. Moreover, he concludes that minorities with the same characteristics were no more likely or less likely to drop out than whites. Dropping out was negatively related to parents' education and income, though the earnings variable was only significant for whites. Student's educational aspirations and ability and the availability of reading material in the home also predicted dropout. All of the factors would tend to increase dropout rates among blacks since they tend to come from lower socioeconomic (SES) backgrounds. Rumburger also found that these characteristics had a greater effect on individuals from lower SES families. For example, among lower SES students, an increase in mothers' education had a greater effect on reducing the chances of dropping out. The effect of childbearing also differed. Young women from higher-income families were less likely to drop out even if they had a child.

A study of Southern low-income teenagers also found blacks at no disadvantage in terms of dropping out once certain variables were controlled. Using data from the Southern Occupational Goals Study, Howell and Frese (1982a,b) examined the relationship between social background, ability, and academic performance and the incidence of teenage parenting, marriage, and dropping out of school. They found that while early parenthood was related to gender (with females more likely to be parents), it was not related to other variables such as race, parent's education or occupation, IQ, or grades. Dropping out was more closely related to these antecedents and whites were more likely to drop out than blacks in this low-income sample. School exit was also more closely linked to early marriage and parenting among whites than among blacks.

Aspirations/Expectations. Our review of the literature on dropping out shows that there are racial differences in dropout rates and that these differences are largely due to differences in socioeconomic backgrounds. However, this information does not tell us whether or not these differences in educational attainment precede or are determined by decisions about sex and contraception. For a better, or more well-rounded, perspective we turn to the literature on educational aspirations and expectations.

Educational aspirations are an indication of the amount of education that an individual would like to have, often without regard to the feasibility of actually obtaining it. Expectations, how much education a person thinks she is likely to obtain, should take account of the obstacles that might prevent an individual from achieving her goal. We reviewed studies on racial differences in educational aspirations to test our hypothesis that differences in educational motivation explain part of the differences in teenage fertility. If we find that blacks have lower aspirations or expectations, then there would be support for our hypothesis. If there are no differences, then we would have to find evidence that young blacks face higher barriers to fulfilling their goals in order to avoid rejecting our hypothesis.

It proved to be difficult to find studies on the educational aspirations and expectations of young women which broke out data by race. Much of the existing literature either focuses on males or on sex differences (mostly among whites). Studies that were available, with the exception of those using the NLS (National Longitudinal Survey), had very small sample sizes and were not national in scope. Therefore, the results should be used cautiously.

The findings from most of the studies indicate that there are no significant racial differences in educational aspirations. Among the unmarried, childless 14- to 17-year-olds enrolled in school in the 1968 NLS, 70 percent of the whites and 71 percent of the blacks aspired to some post-secondary education (Shea, 1971). Of those in the sample who wanted two or more years of college, 90 percent of the whites and 88 percent of the blacks expected to get it. The findings for educational expectations were similar to those found for the 1979 NLS sample (Borus, 1983). This study also found that there appeared to be a leveling process over time with regard to expectations, with individuals from lower socioeconomic backgrounds increasing their expectations and those from higher SES backgrounds lowering their expectations as they got older.

The analysis of the 1979 sample revealed that expectations were positively related to being in a two-parent family and negatively related to number of siblings, having children, and being married. Once social class and family background were controlled for, the study found that minorities expected more education than whites did. The researchers found that black women were more likely to expect to be in the labor force at age 35 but they had slightly higher expectations of a lower status job than white women. Women with children and those who were married had lower educational expectations and lower occupational aspirations, but it was not clear whether this was a cause or a consequence of early parenting and/or marriage.

Studies of black and white adolescent females find very few racial differences in educational and vocational aspirations. George's study (1981) of the occupational aspirations of talented black and white teenagers identified no significant differences by race, although whites from higher socioeconomic backgrounds showed the largest gap between ideal attainment and expectations. Analysis of data from a sample of rural females who were followed over a ten-year period also found few racial differences in educational and occupational aspirations (Kenkel, 1985).

Aspirations/Expectations versus Attainment

While there are few differences in aspirations or expectations, there do appear to be significant gaps between what black females aspire to or expect and the level they actually achieve or might reasonably be expected to achieve. In a study of adolescent life plans, Tittle (1981) found that blacks and Hispanics had higher educational aspirations but these aspirations did not appear to be consistent with their educational programs. For example, 75 percent expected to graduate from college but only 57 percent were enrolled in college preparatory programs.

Kenkel (1985) found similar inconsistencies between occupational aspirations and actual achievement. He examined data from three sets of interviews with low-income rural females. The individuals were first interviewed in 1969 when they were in the fifth and sixth grades. The second interview took place in 1975 when the young women were in high school. The last interview, in 1979, obtained information on actual attainments. Originally 75 percent of the black girls aspired to professional and technical occupations and 71 percent expected to obtain them. The comparable figures for white girls were 70 percent for aspirations and 60 percent for expectations. These figures had dropped considerably by high school, reflecting adjustments to reality. However, white expectations dropped more than those of blacks. In 1979, only 7 percent of blacks and 6 percent of whites actually held professional and technical jobs. While the percentages were equal, the gap between high school expectations and actual achievement was greater for blacks. At the other end of the scale, more whites than blacks had expected to hold low-level jobs but more blacks actually held them.

Several questions arise from these findings. Are young black women more unrealistic in their goals and expectations than young white women? If they are, how does it affect motivation and actual work effort? That is, do they work toward their goals but find their efforts upset by intervening factors outside the educational framework? An alternative explanation also suggests itself. It could be that blacks are not more unrealistic in their goals and expectations, but that they overstate their goals when interviewed in a research study. This could occur if pride would not allow them to admit that they do not expect to achieve certain goals. Here again, it is not clear what effect this has on motivation. Does the same pride motivate the girl to work harder or does she work in accordance with her secret (and lower) expectations? Researchers and survey designers need to direct their attention to restructuring questions on aspirations so that it might be possible to ascertain whether the discrepancies are the result of teenagers' inability to correctly assess their opportunities or their desire to say what they think researchers want to hear.

Determinants of Educational Aspirations and Attainment

Our review of studies on educational aspirations and expectations revealed very little racial difference in the levels of either aspirations or expectations. In fact, most studies indicate that young black women have slightly higher aspirations and expectations than their white counterparts. This undoubtedly reflects the fact that education has long been viewed as the primary means of upward mobility within the black community. It may also reflect a higher expectation of adult labor force participation among blacks, a topic which is explored in more detail in the next chapter. However, even though educational aspirations and expectations are not lower for black women, actual attainment does differ. Although black women are obtaining more education than they have in the past, they are still more likely to drop out of high school than white women (Table 5.2) and are less likely to be enrolled in or to complete college (Table 5.3). The apparent discrepancy between aspirations and attainment appears to lie, in part, in racial differences in background characteristics and educational progress.

One way to get a better perspective on the reality of expectations is to examine the factors that affect aspirations and expectations. As might be expected, a girl's mother plays a large part in her expectations about education and career. The few studies that match mothers and daughters find a strong correlation between mother's education and daughter's aspirations and expectations. A mother's expectations for her daughter are also a factor (Kenkel, forthcoming). One study found that the mother's influence on black females was low at the elementary level but much stronger at the secondary level (Howell and Frese, 1978). These researchers also found that if a mother had children at an early age, her daughter(s) had lower educational expectations. A study of lower class black mothers living in low-income housing found that those with less education (no high school) were more likely to say that they did not care about their daughter's work or education (Jackson, 1981).

Other studies cited in the previous section found that dropout rates, educational aspirations, and educational expectations are related to parents' education, family

TABLE 5.2
Dropout Rates for Young Women Ages 14–19, by Race

Age and Year	White	Black	Black/White Ratio
	%	%	
1970			
14- to 15-year-olds	1.8	2.8	1.6
16- to 17-year-olds	8.4	12.4	1.5
18- to 19-year-olds	14.8	26.6	1.8
1977			
14- to 15-year-olds	1.4	1.5	1.1
16- to 17-year-olds	9.1	8.4	.9
18- to 19-year-olds	14.8	20.3	1.4
1981			
14- to 15-year-olds	2.0	3.0	1.5
16- to 17-year-olds	7.5	8.7	1.2
18- to 19-year-olds	13.2	19.7	1.5

Source: U.S. Bureau of the Census, *School Enrollment—Social and Economic Characteristics of Students*, various years, P-20, Nos. 24, 360, 373.

income, being in a single-parent family, and being two or more years below modal grade. While black women with the same characteristics have educational aspirations and dropout rates similar to whites, it is certainly true that the distribution of these characteristics differs substantially by race.

Young black women come from more disadvantaged backgrounds than young white women. In 1982, 49 percent of black children under the age of 18 lived in single-parent families, compared with 17 percent of white children (U.S. Bureau of the Census, 1983). Since the Census statistics record family status at a given point in time, the number of children who live in a single-parent family for some period of time before they reach age 18 is much larger. In the Shaw study noted earlier (1982), the proportion of the white girls in her sample who had *ever* lived in a single-parent family was 16.4 percent and the proportion of black girls was 42.8 percent. At the time of the survey (1968–73), 9.0 percent of white children and 32 percent of black children were living in single-parent families. As can be seen by Table 5.4, black girls were more likely to be in single-parent families for long periods of time and were more likely to be in them during the high school years. To the extent that being in a single-parent family reduces educational aspirations and increases the chances of dropping out, young black women are at greater risk

TABLE 5.3
Enrollment Status for Women Ages 14–34, by Race

	1971		1981	
	White	Black	White	Black
Not Enrolled,				
Not High School Graduate	%	%	%	%
14 to 15 years old	1.5	1.0	2.0	3.0
16 to 17 years old	8.6	9.2	7.5	8.7
18 to 19 years old	13.8	22.5	13.2	19.7
20 to 21 years old	15.2	25.8	12.8	22.6
22 to 24 years old	17.7	30.0	13.2	17.5
25 to 29 years old	20.4	35.5	12.6	20.5
30 to 34 years old	24.1	40.0	13.6	22.6
Not Enrolled				
High School Graduate				
18 to 19 years old	43.0	34.4	39.0	35.4
20 to 21 years old	57.8	50.1	55.3	74.3
22 to 24 years old	74.2	59.9	73.3	85.3
25 to 29 years old	75.3	60.4	79.5	90.9
30 to 34 years old	72.4	55.8	79.0	92.3
In College				
18 to 19 years old	36.1	22.6	40.1	29.2
20 to 21 years old	26.2	20.8	31.4	23.2
22 to 24 years old	7.7	9.2	12.9	13.1
25 to 29 years old	4.0	2.7	7.6	8.0
30 to 34 years old	3.3	2.8	7.3	6.8

Source: U.S. Bureau of the Census, *School Enrollment—Social and Economic Characteristics of Students*, various years, P-20, Nos. 241, 373.

than their white counterparts (and may be increasingly so if the proportion of black single-parent families continues to increase).

Black children, regardless of family composition, are in families with lower median income and have parents with lower median educational attainment. The 1981 real median income of black married-couple families was only 77 percent of the real median income of white married-couple families, up from 73 percent in 1971. However, virtually all of the gain was among those families in which both parents were working. Black families headed by a woman, an increasing proportion of all black families, had a median income that was only 60 percent of the income of white female-headed families. This is down slightly from 62 percent in 1971. Overall, black families had only 56 percent of the income of white families.

TABLE 5.4
Living Arrangements of Young Women, Ages 14–16, by Race,
1968 NLS Survey

	Race		Black/White Ratio
	White	Black	
	%	%	
Ever Single-parent Family	16.4	42.8	2.6
Single-parent Family for More than 2 Years	11.5	39.1	3.4
Single-parent Family When Daughter Aged 14 to 18	13.9	38.1	2.7

Source: Lois B. Shaw, "High School Completion for Young Women: Effects of Low Income and Living with a Single Parent," *Journal of Family Issues* 3(1982), Table 1.

TABLE 5.5
Educational Attainment of Parents of Young Women
Ages 14–21 in 1979, by Race

Education Completed	Mother		Father	
	White	Black	White	Black
	%	%	%	%
Eight Years or Less	10.7	17.9	16.8	30.5
Nine to Eleven Years	20.6	37.0	16.2	23.6
Twelve Years	47.6	32.7	38.3	31.4
One to Three Years of College	11.6	7.7	10.9	7.9
College Graduate	7.0	3.7	10.4	3.8
Post-Graduate Study	2.4	1.1	7.3	2.9

Source: Urban Institute tabulations from 1979 National Longitudinal Survey of Young Americans.

Although the educational attainment of the black population has increased over the past decade, the parents of young black women continue to have less education that those of young white women. Table 5.5, which uses tabulations from the 1979 NLS, shows that over 50 percent of the parents of the black female respondents had less than a high school education, compared to about 30 percent of the parents of white female respondents. And young black women were only half as likely to have parents who were college graduates. Since parents' educational attainment helps form the educational aspirations of the children and family income is the source of at least some of the funds for postsecondary education, young black women are at a disadvantage compared to their white peers.

Another factor that is associated with a high dropout rate is age-grade lag. High school students who are two or more years behind in school are more likely to drop out. In this area black women have made some progress in the past decade, with rates dropping as much as 50 percent for some ages (Table 5.6), but they still lag behind white women. This probably plays a factor in dropping out, with or without a birth.

Conclusions

In seeking to identify some motivating forces for delayed sex or childbearing among teenagers, the literature on links between education and fertility, on determinants of educational aspirations and attainment, and on racial differences in educational aspirations and expectations was explored. If educational aspirations do affect decisions about sex, contraception, and childbearing and if educational aspirations or expectations differ by race, then these differences may explain at least part of the racial differences in teenage childbearing.

TABLE 5.6
The Percentage of Young Women Who Are Two or More Years
below Modal Grade, by Race

Age and Modal Grade	Percentage of the Enrolled White	Black
1971		
13 years old (Elementary 8)	2.6	4.0
14 years old (High School 1)	3.9	6.9
15 years old (High School 2)	3.4	7.8
16 years old (High School 3)	2.5	5.6
17 years old (High School 4)	2.4	22.5
18 years old (College 1)	4.4	28.9
19 years old (College 2)	8.2	17.1
1979		
13 years old (Elementary 8)	2.6	2.8
14 years old (High School 1)	1.7	4.3
15 years old (High School 2)	1.9	3.9
16 years old (High School 3)	2.9	9.0
17 years old (High School 4)	1.7	8.9
18 years old (College 1)	4.9	10.7
19 years old (College 2)	5.4	11.9

Source: U.S. Bureau of the Census, *School Enrollment—Social and Economic Characteristics of Students*, P-20, Nos. 241, 360.

The available evidence clearly shows a link between educational attainment and fertility among adult women. Within each major racial or ethnic group, women with higher levels of education have fewer children and a smaller expected number of births. Moreover, there is also a link between early childbearing and educational plans. Teenagers with higher educational plans tend to be less likely to have an early birth. Evidence suggests that female teens with high academic aspirations delay sexual activity and pregnancy. This is true for both whites and blacks.

The findings on racial differences in educational aspirations and expectations indicate that in general black and white young women have equally high expectations and that when background factors are statistically controlled, young black women tend to have higher educational aspirations and expectations than young white women. For both races educational plans are affected by parents' education and income, family composition, parental expectations, and educational progress. Since blacks as a group are at a disadvantage in most of these areas, it seems logical to assume that the distribution of educational expectations among young black women differs from that of young white women. In other words, there should be more black women at the low end of the distribution of expectations.

However, the data do not seem to support that conclusion. In both the 1968 and 1979 National Longitudinal Surveys, mean educational aspirations do not differ by race, which suggests that being from a low socioeconomic background does not have as much of a negative effect on the educational aspirations of young black women as it does on young white women. Even though data from the NLS (see Table 5.7) show that background does lower the expected educational attainment, blacks still have educational expectations that are equivalent to those of whites because the magnitude of the background effect on aspirations is lower among blacks.

The racial gap appears in *actual* educational attainment. That is, blacks are less likely to achieve the level of education that they expect to obtain. It is here that the lower socioeconomic backgrounds and the slower rate of educational progress appear to come into play. What is not clear is why blacks are poorer predictors of their educational future. A large proportion of young teenagers seem to be somewhat unrealistic about their likely educational attainment and young black women appear to be somewhat less realistic. Perhaps blacks also underestimate the magnitude of the barriers to achieving their goals. Perhaps they do not give enough weight to the negative effect that low income, parental education, family composition, slow educational progress, and even early childbearing will have on educational attainment. Perhaps failing to see that one's aspirations are unrealistic, and failing to see the real-world factors that affect educational progress undermines the ability

TABLE 5.7
Proportion Aspiring to 16 or More Years of Education by Selected Measures of Family Background and Race: Women Ages 14–17 Enrolled in Elementary or High School, 1968[a]

	Whites	Blacks
Total Family Income, 1967[b]		
$10,000 or more	58	72
Less than $3,000	39	47
Total or Average[c]	48	54
Occupation of Father (or Head of Household) When Respondent was Age 14		
White-collar	62	81
Blue-collar	39	53
Total or average[c]	48	54
Occupation of Mother When Respondent was Age 14[d]		
White-collar	61	70
Blue-collar	42	61
Did not work for pay	48	52
Total or average[c]	48	56
Highest Year of School Completed by Father[e]		
More than 12 years	78	(f)
Less than 12 years	36	61
Total or average[c]	51	57
Highest Year of School Completed by Mother[e]		
More than 12 years	68	81
Less than 12 years	28	49
Total or average[c]	48	54

[a]Includes only nonmarried women with no children.
[b]Includes only respondents living with at least one other family member.
[c]Includes other categories not specified.
[d]Includes only respondents living with their mothers at age 14.
[e]Excludes those whose parent was deceased and those not living with the parent at time of survey or at age 14.
[f]Percentage not shown where base represents fewer than 25 sample cases.
Source: John R. Shea, *Years for Decision: A Longitudinal Study of the Educational and Labor Market Experience of Young Women*, Volume 1, Table 7.3.

of black teens to shape their noneducation behavior to match their educational goals. Alternatively, perhaps the frustration of high aspirations leads to disillusionment, which makes unprotected sex and pregnancy acceptable. Perhaps, as many studies suggest, the role played by aspirations is only important for those with very high aspirations, for example, aspiring to complete college. This would suggest that large numbers of teenagers are motivated or not motivated by other considerations. The state of current research does not make it possible to assess whether any of these hypotheses or any others correctly explain the relationship between education and fertility among black teens. However, it does seem clear that educational aspirations are not lower among black teens and therefore that low aspirations are not the cause of the much higher fertility of high-school-age blacks.

6
Occupational Plans, Job Training and Fertility

Unemployment and Income

Since the mid-1960s black teenage unemployment rates have been about twice as high as those of white teens (see Table 6.1). The recent recession has seen the rate of black teenage unemployment climb to the 40 percent range, and the gap between their job holding chances and those of white teens has grown even larger. Unemployment rates of adult blacks, consistently about twice as high as those of whites, also increased during the recession more than those of white adults.

Recent data on median family income by race show that the gap between black and white incomes diminished during the period of the late 1960s to mid-1970s and quickly deteriorated during the recession of the mid-1970s. Median black family incomes in 1982 stood in about the same relationship to white family income as it had in 1960 (see Table 6.2).

Employment and Fertility

The cross-sectional association between employment and fertility is very strong (see Table 6.3). Women who are employed and working women with higher status occupations tend to have fewer children and they are more likely to be childless. This basic association holds among white women, black women, and Spanish-origin women. While the relationship is clear, the causal process underlying the association is not equally obvious. It may be explained by a tendency on the part of career-oriented women to delay childbearing or by a tendency among women who do not have children for other reasons to proceed further with their schooling and then move into relatively demanding occupations. Some researchers have found that employed wives want fewer children and thus limit their fertility (Pratt and Whelpton, 1956; Ridley, 1959; Whelpton et al., 1966). Women who plan to work also anticipate smaller families than those with no work expectations (Blake, 1970; Farley, 1970; Stolzenberg and Waite, 1977). Other researchers have found that the number and ages of children help explain whether a woman chooses to work (Freedman et al., 1959; Sweet, 1973). Studies that allow for reciprocity between em-

TABLE 6.1
Unemployment Rates by Race and Age, Selected Years

	White		Black and Other	
	Ages 16 - 19	Ages 20 and over	Ages 16 - 19	Ages 20 and over
1955	10.3	3.4	15.8	7.5
1960	13.4	4.1	10.2	9.1
1965	13.4	3.3	26.2	6.2
1970	13.5	3.7	29.1	6.1
1975	17.9	6.7	36.7	11.6
1980	15.5	5.4	35.4	11.2
1981	17.3	5.4	37.8	12.2
1982	17.3	7.6	41.4	16.6

Source: U.S. Department of Labor, "Employment and Training Report of the President," 1982; and "Employment and Earnings," January 1983.

TABLE 6.2
Median Family Income In Constant (1982) Dollars by Race, Selected Years

	Black	White	Ratio
1960	$10,528[a]	$19,018	.554[a]
1970	15,608	25,445	.613
1975	15,744	25,589	.615
1980	14,846	25,658	.579
1981	14,079	24,959	.564
1982	13,598	24,603	.553

[a]Data for black and other races. Median black family income was approximately 96 percent as high as that for black and other races during the early 1970s, suggesting the data for 1960 overstate black median family income by some undetermined amount.

Source: U.S. Department of Commerce, Bureau of the Census, Money Income and Poverty Status of Families and Persons in the United States: 1982, P-60, No. 140.

ployment and fertility decisions have not fully resolved the issue. Current research suggests that a birth has a negative impact on employment in the short run but that in the long run childbearing is reduced to accommodate plans for employment (Cramer, 1980; Hofferth, 1981; Smith-Lovin and Tickamyer, 1978; Waite and Stolzenberg, 1976; Hout, 1978).

TABLE 6.3
Children Ever Born and Percent Childless among Women Ages 25–34 in 1981, by Race and Ethnicity

	Children Born Per 1,000 Women			Percent Childless		
	White	Black	Spanish Origin[a]	White	Black	Spanish Origin[a]
Occupation						
Professional/ Technical	639	} 1,197	893	61.5	} 42.3	43.4
Managers/ Administrators	832			51.3		
Sales workers	1,162	} 1,454	1,500	37.3	} 27.8	25.5
Clerical workers	1,082			40.7		
Blue-collar workers	1,515	2,010	1,959	24.7	14.3	17.9
Service workers	1,467	1,999	1,458	28.9	20.9	29.3
Labor Force Status						
Women in labor force	1,110	1,689	1,537	41.3	25.0	27.0
Employed	1,084	1,623	1,506	42.2	26.8	27.7
Unemployed	1,508	2,053	—	27.5	15.2	—
Women not in labor force	2,008	2,587	2,544	9.8	11.5	7.5

[a]Persons of Spanish origin may be of any race.

Source: U.S. Bureau of the Census, *Fertility of American Women: June 1981*, Current Population Reports, series P-20, no. 378, Table 12.

Despite the plethora of studies on labor force attachment and fertility among adult women, very little research has been conducted on the effect of employment and employment aspirations on the fertility behavior of teenagers and the results of the available research are quite mixed. Waite and Spitze (1980) analyzing the National Longitudinal Survey of Young Women, find that women who plan to work when they are 35 years of age are less likely to have a birth through their early twenties and that work plans have a significant negative effect among teens aged 16 and 17. Using the same data, however, McLaughlin (1981) does not find a similar association, perhaps because of the very delimited dependent variable he used—whether a birth occurred 9 to 21 months after the interview. McLaughlin also differentiated among occupations that have lengthy training requirements and those that do not, but he still did not find that aspirations for an occupation requiring a high investment of preparation time predict a lower probability of having a birth as a teenager.

In a related study using the NLS, Cherlin (1980) found that women who expected to work outside the home at age 35 were substantially more likely to postpone marriage, except for younger black women. Moore (1980) using the 1976 Survey of Income and Occupation (SIE) found only weak and inconsistent support for the hypotheses that young women residing in areas with high unemployment rates among youth of their race and sex had higher fertility or that higher wages for young women predict lower fertility. Since the SIE turned out to have an undercount of births to teens, this hypothesis should be explored using other data. Only one such analysis has been found. Field (1981) estimated a three-stage least squares analysis of the determinants of the teenage out-of-wedlock birth rate in SMSAs using a macroeconomic approach. He found that the proportion of teens employed at least 26 weeks in 1970 to be negatively and significantly related to the 1971 out-of-wedlock birth rate. However, higher median annual income among employed women over 13 was positively related to out-of-wedlock fertility. Unfortunately, separate analyses were not done for blacks and whites.

Howell and Frese (1982) used longitudinal data on a low-income Southern sample to explore this issue. Neither parental nor youth occupational aspirations were found to predict parenthood during the high school years. Unfortunately males and females were aggregated and no interaction terms were included, so the possibility that aspirations only affect female fertility was not examined. Nevertheless, this is the only study to include males in the sample at all.

Interestingly, we have discovered no studies that specifically explore the relationship between the occupational plans of male teenagers and their fertility-related behaviors. Since the occurrence of an untimely birth is more likely to interfere with a young woman's plans than a young man's plans, this difference is not unexpected. Yet it is frequently suggested that one factor pressing young males toward fathering a child is the lack of other ways to acquire adult status and self-esteem. While virtually none of the black youth interviewed in our small survey of high school students indicated that the absence of good jobs would be a motivation for initiating a pregnancy either for a boy or a girl, feeling grown up was frequently mentioned, particularly as a reason boys have for getting a girl pregnant. A third of the girls and 12 percent of the boys selected the desire to feel grown up as the primary reason boys get girls pregnant.

Given the paucity of research on this important question, further work is warranted; however it is necessary to think through in greater detail what effects might be anticipated. Perhaps no impact should be anticipated for those males who see no prospect of a forced marriage; on the other hand, male aspirations might be associated with efforts to avoid pregnancy if pregnancy is expected to result in marriage. Marriage expectations are presumably related to the type of relationship. Males in casual relationships may see little prospect of marriage, and thus feel few personal implications if a pregnancy occurs. Males in close relationships may anticipate greater personal consequences. They may also better perceive and feel greater concern about consequences for the female's life if they are involved in a close relationship. Such an association could account in part for the finding that contraceptive use is more common in committed relationships. Not only is sex more predictable, but the human consequences of an unwanted pregnancy may be of greater concern to both partners.

Expecting to work may also be a different variable for different women. Black women, for example, are more likely to anticipate employment when they are 35 than are white women (Cherlin, 1980), but this expectation may not reflect greater career commitment. Black women may simply be stating that on the basis of their own experience and that of others that they see, a woman is likely to need to work through her thirties. As Hamilton and Crouter (1980) note, work may be alienating rather than fulfilling. In fact, Macke and Morgan (1978) have found that black girls often reacted negatively to having a mother who had been employed, given the low status occupations that many black women have. Thus employment expectations may not be a positive force, a goal for which current satisfactions are to be foregone.

Among very young teens, moreover, employment aspirations may be only partly formed and they may be highly unrealistic. Stolzenberg and Waite (1977) have found that the statistical correlation between young women's labor force plans and their fertility expectations is much larger among women in their middle and late twenties than it is for women aged 19 to 20. They marshal considerable evidence indicating that the association becomes stronger over time because of women's increasing realization as they age that small families are more compatible with labor force participation. Presumably teens less than 18 may hold highly unrealistic notions about employment and fertility.

The high rates of unemployment experienced by black youth and the relative disparities in adult blacks' employment and earnings compared to whites' do not seem to have affected the majority of black teens' aspirations. As Table 6.4 indicates, black occupational aspirations are as high as those of whites among males and higher than whites among females (Borus, 1983). However, many black youths like many white youths do not seem to be aware that early childbearing may hinder their ability to achieve their goals.

There are two possible reasons for this: first, black youth, like youth in general, may believe that they are invulnerable to the misfortunes of their

TABLE 6.4

Desired Activity—Occupation Group at Age 35, by Sex, Race, and Ethnicity; Percentage Distributions

Occupation	Female			Male			
	Black	Hispanic	White	Black	Hispanic	White	Total
White collar	64	54	53	52	47	52	53
High status[a]	46	36	41	48	45	49	45
Low status[b]	19	18	12	4	2	2	8
Blue collar	4	3	4	31	32	28	16
High status[c]	1	1	2	17	21	19	10
Low status[d]	3	2	2	14	11	9	6
Service	10	8	7	2	4	3	5
Farmers and farm workers	0	0	0	1	2	3	1
Working, occupations not specified	1	2	2	2	2	1	2
Don't know	8	10	8	10	11	12	10
Home (out of labor force)	12	23	26	2	2	2	13
Total percentage	100	100	100	100	100	100	100

[a]Professional, technical, and kindred workers; managers and administrators (nonfarm).
[b]Sales workers; clerical and kindred workers.
[c]Craftspersons and kindred workers.
[d]Operatives and nonfarm laborers.

Source: D. Shapiro and J. Crowley, "Hopes and Plans: Education, Work Activity and Fertility," in M. Borus, ed., *Tomorrow's Workers* (Lexington, Mass.: Lexington Books, 1983), Table 5-4.

Universe: Civilians ages 14–21 on January 1, 1979, National Longitudinal Survey of Youth.

elders. Youth, often with the urging of their elders, have ambitions to outstrip the accomplishments of the preceding generation. Thus, we observe high aspirations for education and living standards among teenagers of all races.

At the same time, the evidence indicates that black youth are particularly susceptible to obstacles that will impede the achievement of their dreams. Early childbearing is one of the obstacles, as we have seen. Other obstacles include low socioeconomic status that may lead to various personal and family crises that ultimately result in delaying or frustrating the accomplishment of individual goals. Finally, racism may also play a part to the extent that black teenagers' efforts to achieve in school, at work, or socially are frustrated because of racial prejudice.

Given the realities that black teenagers face, one is tempted to characterize their aspirations as idealistic or unrealistic. But, perhaps fortunately for black teenagers, this view can only be arrived at after studying the outcomes experienced by thousands (if not millions) of blacks. Most teens do not have a fatalistic view of their futures, but neither do they have a mature understanding of what is necessary for them to reach their goals.

Numerous studies have attempted to ascertain the impact that the availability of income maintenance payments have on work effort. The consensus of this literature, involving personal interviews and analysis of data from social experiments in several geographical areas, is that most people prefer to work than to accept welfare (SRI, 1983).

Clearly, youth are no exception. They typically have very high (if unrealistic) expectations about their job and earnings opportunities. At the same time, recent studies indicate black youth have a strong willingness to work at wage rates and jobs that are less attractive than they thought they could obtain (Borus et al., 1980). In addition, youth are likely to view welfare benefits as being inadequate to support themselves and their families. A recent study of teenage mothers involved in Project Redirection asked them whether they became pregnant to obtain welfare benefits. Only one or two out of eighteen said that obtaining their own welfare grant was a goal (Levy with Grinker, 1983).

Thus, like their white counterparts, the vast majority of black teenagers maintain high aspirations for their future; a future that involves more education, a better job, and a higher standard of living than that of their parents. The tragedy of teenage pregnancy is that it may significantly hinder the attainment of those aspirations, especially for disadvantaged youth.

Aspirations and expectations for employment may simply be too distant in time and reality to affect teenagers' current fertility behavior. Loken and Fishbein (1980) report that even among married childless women, all work variables have only an indirect effect on childbearing intentions; the effect is transmitted through their effects on attitudes toward having a child and their subjective norms. We expect that this is true for teens as well—that attitudes toward marriage and family and having a child and whether having a child can or should interfere with employment confound any direct impact of occupational aspirations on fertility. However, we expect that among teenagers something more is at work, or perhaps it is more accurate to say that something is not at work. Teenagers do not reason like adults. They lack experience in life and they often lack the cognitive maturity to reason abstractly and to see connections between current behavior and distant outcomes. This is true for many adults as well, but Stolzenberg and Waite (1977) have found that the consistency of young women's occupational and fertility plans increases as the young women age, suggesting the there is a learning or developmental increase associated with getting older. Among teens who initiate sexual activity during junior high, it may simply be too much to expect even those youths with high aspirations to rationally weigh the risks they are taking and act accordingly. Researchers and social workers concerned about early drug use, smoking, reckless driving, and runaways are presumably confronting the same lack of experience and cognitive maturity among youth. Unfortunately, these issues are typically studied as separate problem behaviors. Studying successful interventions oriented toward delaying drug use or smoking might be applicable to efforts to delay the initiation of sexual activity to an age at which youth have acquired sufficient experience and cognitive maturity to appreciate the consequences of their behavior.

Job Training Programs

During fiscal year 1980 approximately $4.2 billion was spent serving youth in federal employment and training programs, according to data from the Congressional Budget Office. While there are numerous components to training programs, to the extent that they increase skill levels of participants or increase their marketability they affect their prospective earnings and hence may affect their behavior with regard to fertility, marriage, school attendance, educational attainment, and employment and earnings.

We will briefly review what is known about the effect of training program participation on fertility and then consider other effects of training programs.

First, it is clear that fertility decreases young women's participation in employment and skills-training programs. Simms and Leitch (1983) found that having dependents decreased the probability of participating in a post-1978 government training program for youths in the 1979 NLS sample. While they found the magnitude of the effect of having dependents was larger for females, it was found that having dependents decreased the participation of males by a sizeable amount as well.

Having established the fact that young mothers are less likely to participate in conventional employment and training programs, we turn now to an assessment of the impact of training program participation on fertility.

Fertility Impacts

Only limited information is available on the effects of training program participation on fertility. In theory, if there were any effect of participation on fertility it would reflect the fact that increased earnings due to participation increase the demand for children while increased wage rates due to participation reduce the demand for children, because market work is substituted for child-rearing as the opportunity cost of childrearing (wage rate) rises. Since these effects operate in opposite directions there is no way to know *a priori* the effect of training program participation on fertility. However, several researchers have found that the effect of opportunity costs may outweigh the income effect (Mallar et al., 1980; Groenevald, 1980). Furthermore, even if it can be shown that participating in a program reduces fertility, given the short-term nature of most programs it is possible that participation delays births rather than affecting completed family size. (There is some evidence, however, that there is a positive association between delaying births and reducing completed family size; see Moore and Burt, 1982.)

One of the few studies of a federal employment and training program that explicitly considered the issue of fertility was a study of Job Corps (Mallar et al., 1980). Job Corps is a largely residential program offering skills training to disadvantaged out-of-school youth aged 14 to 21. Youth who participated in the program in 1977 were followed up eighteen months after leaving the program, and compared to similar nonparticipants. Women enrollees showed differential postprogram experience depending on whether or not they were mothers. Job Corps participation helped nonmothers more than mothers in terms of increased employment and earnings. At the same time, there is an indication that 18 months after leaving the program, Job Corps participation reduced the number of births by 14 percent, and lowered illegitimacy rates by 4 percent for all women participants relative to the comparison group. Job Corps also lowered marriage rates by 6 to 9 percent for women participants. Thus while Job Corps may have benefitted nonmothers more initially, the effects of Job Corps on family formation and fertility suggest that women who entered the program with children may receive a long-run positive effect that could not be fully measured 18 months after program termination. The evidence also suggests that participation decreased fertility among males by 2 to 3 percent relative to males in the comparison group. While the effects for males were smaller in magnitude than those for women and generally insignificant, this is one of the few studies of which we are aware that addresses this issue (Mallar et al., 1980).

Unfortunately, the female comparison group may not have been well matched in terms of child responsibility status. Thus, while over the entire study period female Corps members with children represented 9 percent of the participant sample, in the first six months after participation they represented only 2 percent of the sample but were 15 percent of the sample during the last six months of the study period (at which time approximately 50 percent of female participants had children present). Nonparticipant women with children constituted 27 percent of the comparison group sample during the postprogram study period, but data are not provided on their childbearing at other points during the study period. Based on what is known about the difference in average rates of childbearing between the two groups over the study period and the fact that participant women's children tended to be young, we must assume that childbearing rates among comparison group women were initially higher than those for participants. This assumption is also consistent with the evidence on the effect of fertility on participation in programs, particularly one like Job Corps which requires relocation to a residential setting that may be far removed from the normal home environment.

Thus, the Job Corps results pertaining to fertility and family formation should be treated as only suggestive. They may reflect the fact that women who chose to participate in Job Corps were more highly motivated than average and had decided to postpone childbearing and marriage. Therefore, the outcomes may reflect the results of self-selection of highly motivated young women rather than program-induced effects.

The Supported Work program, a large-scale, multi-year demonstration effort designed to test the effectiveness of a structured work experience program for long-term female AFDC beneficiaries, ex-addicts, ex-offenders, and young school dropouts, provided participants with 12 to 18 months of employment, counseling, and supervision. An evaluation of the program impacts 27 months after participants enrolled (i.e., 9 to 15 months after leaving) showed significant savings in transfer payments (AFDC, Food Stamps, etc.) particularly for AFDC mothers. AFDC mothers experienced gains in hourly wage rates, hours worked, and earned income that were significantly higher than those experienced by the randomly assigned control group. While in theory some part of the reduction in the receipt of AFDC and other transfer income might be due to reduced fertility of the Supported Work participants, there is little indication that this occurred. The lack of a fertility effect may be due to the relatively high average age (33.6 years) of the female AFDC program participants (MDRC, 1980).

Finally, results from an experimental program designed to test the effects of replacing the current welfare system with a combination of a negative income tax and various manpower program offerings found a 31 percent reduction in fertility during the second and third years of the program among single black women assigned to the manpower counseling treatment, while the program offering a 50 percent subsidy of training/education costs appears to have reduced single black women's fertility by 49 percent below that of controls (Groenevald, 1980). The experimental results for Chicano and white women were less consistent, probably due in part to limitations of the data that do not permit distinctions among actual participants and those who were only offered the "treatment" but did not avail themselves of it. At the same time, negative effects on fertility among single black women are consistently found.

Training Program Impacts on Earnings and Employment

One of the few efforts to examine the impact of employment and training efforts on young women that explicitly considered whether they had children was again in connection with Job Corps. Study results indicated that up to 24 months after leaving the program, young women without children had significantly higher earnings ($14 per week) and were significantly more likely to be in the labor force (11 percent) and to be employed in a union job (5 percent) than similar nonparticipants.

Women with children evidenced no significant differences in outcomes from their comparison group counterparts except for a higher percentage of time spent in a training program (1.8 percent) or in college (1.6 percent). Again the nature of the comparison group precludes firm reliance on these estimated effects.

Most of the efforts to evaluate the impact of employment and training programs have not focused on youth. In fact, a recent Urban Institute project is one of the few studies of which we are aware that attempts to take a comprehensive look at how youth (male or female) fared in federal employment and training efforts during the 1970s. Findings from the net impact analysis indicated that many of the programs that worked for adults also worked for youth. Public Service Employment (PSE) and on-the-job training (OJT) had significant earnings effects for young women, most notably minority women, with net gains in annual earnings ranging from $600 to $1900. Unlike adults, classroom training and work experience did not lead to net earnings gains for youth. The analysis showed that the postprogram labor force activity of youthful CETA participants was substantially higher than their preprogram activity in terms of time in the labor force, time employed, and hours worked. This is true even of individuals in programs, such as youth work experience, that showed no earnings gains compared to the match groups. Since we lacked comparable data for the match group, we could not determine the extent to which these gains in labor market activity by CETA participants differed from those of nonparticipants. Among those groups showing net earnings gains, most of the gain is attributable to increased labor market activity and not increased hourly wages.

Programs Directed at Teen Mothers

Whether to participate in job training or to reenroll in high school if one has not completed high school is a difficult choice for teenagers in general. Teenage mothers must also consider the need to make arrangements for child care. In addition, the burdens of attending school or participating in training in most cases must be added to their current responsibilities as a mother.

These realities help to explain the low rates of participation in training programs for women with young children. Job Corps, as discussed previously, presents an added complication because of its largely residential nature. Thus, in order to participate, young mothers must find someone to take full responsibility for the child over a period of several months.

While these factors inhibit participation, it is true that without the necessary skills to earn an adequate income, many teenage mothers are likely to become dependent on welfare and/or have additional children.

Numerous public and private efforts targeted on teenage mothers have been developed over the past few years. In 1980, 26 projects were funded by the Office of Adolescent Pregnancy Programs (OAPP) in the Department of Health and Human Services to develop supportive services for pregnant and parenting teens pursuant to P.L. 95-626. The OAPP projects offered a variety of services to pregnant and parenting teens (including male partners in some instances). The services offered included family planning counseling, educational counseling, day care, and transportation services, with different sites providing different service mixes.

Preliminary results of a major study of these programs indicate that relative to various control and comparison groups, OAPP project participants experienced increased school completion rates, reduced probability of a repeat pregnancy (over a one- to two-year period), reduced welfare dependency among clients who had been in the program the longest, but less employment and less training program participation (see Table 6.5) (Kimmich et al., 1983).

Another program, Project Redirection, jointly funded by the Ford Foundation and the U.S. Department of Labor, was designed to test whether providing pregnant and parenting teens with counseling and supportive services would affect their rates of school completion, fertility, employment and welfare dependency. Results of a 12-month follow-up indicate that project participants were less likely to experience a repeat pregnancy and were more likely to remain in high school or participate in a training program than similar nonparticipants.

Results for employment outcomes indicate that participants were slightly more likely to be in the labor force 12 months following program entry

TABLE 6.5
Teen Parent Outcomes

	OAPP-Funded Projects	Project Redirection[a] Experimentals	Project Redirection[a] Comparison	Mott & Maxwell[b]
Pregnant again within 1 to 12 months of last baby's birth				
Clients delivering in program	15%	--	--	--
Clients entering with baby	17%	17%	22%	--
Pregnant again within 1-24 months of last baby's birth				
Clients delivering in program	34%	--	--	--
Clients entering with baby	30%	--	--	--
In or completed school program at delivery (pregnant clients only)	71%	--	--	62% Whites 71% Blacks
Within 1-12 months of last baby's birth:				
Clients delivering in program	62%	--	--	58% Whites 61% Blacks
Clients entering with baby	61%	66%	50%	--
Within 1-24 months of last baby's birth:				
Clients delivering in program	60%	--	--	--
Clients entering with baby	55%	--	--	--
In or completed job training program				
Within 1-12 months of last baby's birth:				
Clients delivering in program	12%	34%	21%	--
Clients entering with baby	12%	--	--	--
Within 1-24 months of last baby's birth:				
Clients delivering in program	12%	--	--	--
Clients entering with baby	21%	--	--	--
Welfare status--not receiving any public support:				
At 12 months after last baby's birth:				
Clients delivering in program	39%	20%	--	White 77% graduates 68% dropouts
Clients entering with baby	39%	--	--	Black 55% graduates 26% dropouts
Employment status at 12 months				
Employment to population ratio (E/P)	19.3%	15.1%	17.1%	32.6%
Labor force participation rate (L/P)	34.1%	61.5%	54.0%	51.3%
Unemployment rate (U/L)	43.1%	75.5%	67.8%	36.5%

[a]Denise F. Polit, et al. *School, Work and Family Planning* (Manpower Demonstration Research Corp., 1983).
[b]Frank L. Mott and Nan L. Maxwell, "School-Age Mothers: 1968 and 1979," *Family Planning Perspectives* (1981).
Source: Kimmich et al., *Helping Pregnant Adolescents* (Washington, D.C.: The Urban Institute, 1983).

compared to controls. Program participants were also twice as likely as controls to be employed full-time, but only one-half as likely to be employed part-time. This result appears to be related to the fact that Project Redirection participants were significantly more likely than controls to be enrolled in or have completed high school or a GED program at the 12-month follow-up, and less likely than controls to work part-time while in school.

It is difficult to evaluate the significance of these results for several reasons. At the time of the 12-month interview many teens were still participating in the program or had only recently left. All Project Redirection participants were WIN-eligible at entry, and the WIN program requires that participants make a meaningful effort to find employment. Since Redirection did not gather data on receipt of welfare in the 12-month interview, it is not possible to determine whether differences in continued participation in WIN account for differences in job seeking. Evaluation results for program participants at 24 months post partum are expected to be available in the near future.

As Table 6.5 indicates, the services provided under OAPP programs appear to have had a greater effect on increasing employment rates for those in the labor force than Project Redirection, while at the same time, Project Redirection comparisons and experimentals were more likely to be in the labor force.

The Mott and Maxwell comparison groups exhibited generally better labor force outcomes than any of the program groups. This may be largely due to the older ages (up to age 22) of the mothers in the Mott-Maxwell sample, and the fact that there was no control for ages of children. By contrast, labor force experience for the OAPP and Redirection participants was ascertained when their youngest child was probably between six months and two years old.

While the evidence on employment outcomes is not as encouraging as might be hoped for, other findings for a variety of programs directed towards pregnant and parenting teens consistently indicate that outcomes related to schooling, training, fertility, and (to some extent) welfare dependence, can be positively affected by service provision.

In addition to the relatively short-term gains that may be apparent with respect to schooling and receipt of public support, longer-term gains due to lower fertililty as well as increased schooling and training program participation would be realized as work experience increases.

If these programs are helpful to teenagers who have become mothers, there might be preventive value in early involvement in job training programs.

Conclusions

In summary, the literature on employment aspirations and fertility among teens is thin for females and nonexistent for males. The studies that have explored this issue among young females have produced inconclusive results. Occupational plans and opportunities may well affect fertility behavior, but the direct evidence is weak. Many reasons can be advanced to explain the lack of a strong effect, for example, lack of awareness of the requirements of the world of work. Also numerous variables can be suggested that might interact with occupational plans, for example, level of career commitment. Given the paucity of information in general, race-specific effects can only be the subject of speculation. Furthermore, given evidence that black occupational aspirations are as high as whites, it seems unlikely that low aspirations provide a ready explanation for the high rate of adolescent pregnancy among blacks.

It seems likely, however, that the impact of occupational aspirations will be smaller than the impact of educational aspirations since school is more salient to school-age youth. Since we have tentatively concluded that the direct effect of educational aspirations is strong only when aspirations are very high, a strong general effect is not anticipated. But more subtle and indirect effects may well be documented. For example, the experience of frequent unemployment may not lower but raise aspirations among youth, perhaps unrealistically, while also producing less trust in marriage as a dependable source of support. Many service providers comment that they encounter teens who are apathetic because they feel they have no future (e.g., Hoffner, 1983), but researchers have not documented this effect.

The results of several studies of youth enrolled in job training programs are somewhat encouraging, though tentative. It may be the case that program recruits are particularly motivated, but, compared to comparison groups, youth who complete job training programs seem to have lower fertility.

7

Marriage and Family

Marriage Patterns

Just as striking as the high incidence of early childbearing among blacks is the extent to which these births occur outside of marriage. At 64 percent, the proportion of births to black teens that occurred outside of marriage was already high in 1970. Yet this proportion continued to rise during the 1970s and by 1982, 87 percent of the births to black teens were out-of-wedlock. The same trend has occurred among black women over the age of 20, but the absolute proportion is only about half as great. Among black women over 20, 47 percent of all births were out-of-wedlock in 1982, compared to 26 percent in 1970.

The proportion of births occurring outside of marriage increased among whites between 1970 and 1982 as well—from 17 percent to 38 percent among teenagers and from 4 percent to 9 percent among women 20 and older. Thus part of the change in black patterns aligns with the general trend in the United States (and in many European countries). However, the proportion of births among U.S. blacks occurring outside marriage is particularly high, suggesting that it is more than a simple reflection of general societal trends. In addition, black marriage patterns in and of themselves differ from those of whites and Spanish-origin Americans.

Marriage is uncommon among teenagers under age 18, regardless of race; but it is least common among black teens (see Table 7.1). Spanish-origin females, white females, and Spanish-origin males are more likely to be married at a young age, a pattern that becomes quite strong by ages 18 and 19. As of 1982 a quarter of Spanish-origin females and 12 percent of Spanish-origin males had married before the age of 20. Sixteen percent of white females and 6 percent of white males had married. However, only 4 percent of black females and just over 1 percent of black males had married before the age of 20 in 1980. In 1970, over a quarter of the black females aged 18-19 had married, indicating a rapid change in marriage patterns in just a dozen years. The change among white females was not nearly as dramatic. Data for 1970 are not available for Spanish-origin teens. Comparing blacks and whites,

TABLE 7.1
Percent Never Married, by Age, Sex and Race, 1970 and 1982, and by
Ethnicity, 1982

| | Age | | | | | | | |
| | 14/15 - 17[a] | | 18 - 19 | | 20 - 24 | | 25 - 29 | |
	1982	1970	1982	1970	1982	1970	1982	1970
Males								
All races	99.3	99.3	94.9	92.5	72.0	55.2	36.1	19.7
White	99.3	99.3	94.2	92.0	70.1	54.5	34.1	17.9
Black	99.6	99.5	98.7	95.8	82.3	59.4	48.3	32.0
Spanish origin[b]	98.8	--	87.8	--	65.6	--	31.1	--
Females								
All Races	97.2	97.3	84.9	75.5	53.4	35.9	23.4	10.7
White	96.8	97.2	83.1	75.5	50.5	34.7	20.6	9.5
Black	98.8	98.2	96.0	73.9	71.5	43.3	40.6	19.0
Spanish origin[b]	94.1	--	74.4	--	44.7	--	20.3	--

[a]1970 age category is 14–17; 1982 age is 15–17.
[b]Persons of Spanish origin may be of any race.
Source: U.S. Bureau of the Census, "Marital Status and Family Status: March 1970," Current
Population Reports, P-20, No. 212, Table 1; "Marital Status and Living Arrangements:
March 1982," P-20, No. 380, Table 1.

though, it can be seen that comparable proportions of teens were married in
1970, but a substantial gap had occurred by 1982.

It is important to recognize the recency of the current situation. Long-
standing differences have existed, but not of the current magnitude. Data on
marital status according to age and race for the years 1970 and 1982, shown
in Tables 7.2 and 7.3, illustrate the significant changes that have occurred
during the last dozen years.

Among women under the age of 25, sharp declines in the proportion who
are married and living with their husband have occurred for both whites and
blacks (see Table 7.2). The drop has been far steeper among blacks, though,
from 21 to 3 percent at ages 18 to 19, compared with a decline from 21 to
14 percent among whites. At ages 20 to 24, a decline from 43 to 22 percent
occurred compared with a decline from 58 to 42 percent among whites.

In 1970, most black women over the age of 25 were married. By 1982,
there was no age category of black females in which a majority of the women

TABLE 7.2

Marital Status Distribution by Age and Race, 1982 and 1970, and by Spanish Origin, 1970; Males 18–44

	1982						1970					
	18-19	20-24	25-29	30-34	35-39	40-44	18-19	20-24	25-29	30-34	35-39	40-44
All Races												
Single	94.9	72.0	36.1	17.3	10.0	7.4	92.5	55.2	19.7	9.6	7.6	6.9
Married, wife present	3.7	24.9	54.7	69.7	76.8	79.3	6.8	41.5	75.2	84.4	86.3	85.6
Separated	1.2	1.8	3.2	3.6	3.1	3.9	0.6	2.1	2.8	3.0	3.0	3.7
Widowed	—	—	—	0.1	0.2	0.5	—	—	0.1	0.1	0.4	0.8
Divorced	0.1	1.3	6.0	9.2	9.8	8.9	—	1.1	2.3	2.9	2.7	3.0
Whites												
Single	94.2	70.1	34.1	16.5	8.8	7.2	92.0	54.5	17.9	9.4	6.6	6.3
Married, wife present	4.2	26.6	56.8	71.2	79.4	80.3	7.4	42.6	77.5	85.6	89.1	87.9
Separated	1.4	1.9	3.0	3.1	2.5	3.1	0.6	1.9	2.1	2.2	1.8	2.5
Widowed	—	—	—	0.1	0.2	0.5	—	—	0.1	0.1	0.3	0.6
Divorced	0.2	1.4	6.1	9.1	9.2	8.9	0.1	1.0	2.4	2.7	2.2	2.8
Blacks												
Single	98.7	82.3	48.3	23.2	21.7	9.4	95.8	59.4	32.0	9.5	15.3	11.8
Married, wife present	0.7	15.7	40.7	56.9	51.2	68.5	3.0	35.3	57.7	75.3	62.7	66.1
Separated	0.6	1.6	4.8	8.0	8.7	11.0	1.4	3.8	8.4	10.1	13.6	15.0
Widowed	—	—	0.2	0.4	0.5	—	—	0.2	—	0.6	1.8	2.7
Divorced	—	0.4	6.1	11.6	18.0	11.1	—	1.5	1.9	4.6	6.6	4.4
Spanish Origin[a]												
Single	87.8	65.6	31.1	11.7	10.4	5.0						
Married, wife present	7.7	29.7	58.6	75.7	77.7	81.5						
Separated	4.4	3.8	6.3	4.9	4.7	7.8						
Widowed	—	—	—	0.1	0.5	—						
Divorced	—	0.9	4.1	7.5	6.6	5.7						

[a]Persons of Spanish origin may be of any race.

Source: U.S. Bureau of the Census, "Marital Status and Family Status: March 1970," P-20, no. 212, Table 1; "Marital Status and Living Arrangements: March 1982," Current Population Reports, P-20, no. 380, Table 1.

TABLE 7.3

Marital Status Distribution by Age and Race, 1982 and 1970, and by Spanish Origin, 1970; Females 18–44

	1982						1970					
	18–19	20–24	25–29	30–34	35–39	40–44	18–19	20–24	25–29	30–34	35–39	40–44
All Races												
Single	84.9	53.4	23.4	11.6	6.4	4.7	75.5	35.9	10.7	6.4	5.5	5.0
Married, wife present	12.5	39.0	62.1	70.3	73.2	74.3	20.8	56.0	79.7	83.5	83.3	82.3
Separated	2.0	3.9	5.2	5.3	6.0	5.4	3.4	5.4	4.9	4.7	4.2	4.0
Widowed	—	0.1	0.5	0.7	1.5	3.5	—	0.3	0.3	0.8	1.8	3.1
Divorced	0.7	3.5	8.8	12.1	13.0	12.1	—	2.3	4.3	4.6	5.2	5.5
Whites												
Single	83.1	50.5	20.6	10.0	5.0	4.0	75.5	34.7	9.5	5.7	4.7	4.8
Married, wife present	14.1	41.7	65.6	73.7	76.7	77.5	20.9	58.0	82.5	86.5	86.9	84.6
Separated	2.1	3.9	4.4	4.1	4.4	3.7	3.1	4.6	3.6	2.6	2.5	2.7
Widowed	—	0.1	0.5	0.5	1.2	3.0	—	0.3	0.3	0.6	1.2	2.6
Divorced	0.8	3.8	9.0	11.7	12.7	11.9	0.4	2.4	4.1	4.6	4.8	5.3
Blacks												
Single	96.8	71.5	40.6	23.3	16.9	10.1	73.9	43.3	19.0	10.8	12.2	56.8
Married, wife present	2.7	22.3	39.7	44.8	45.7	49.3	21.0	42.6	59.7	61.3	54.8	61.8
Separated	1.3	4.2	10.9	14.4	18.3	18.7	5.0	12.2	15.4	20.5	17.9	15.8
Widowed	—	0.2	0.5	1.8	3.5	6.8	—	0.4	0.3	2.0	6.6	7.9
Divorced	—	1.8	8.3	15.6	15.6	15.0	0.2	1.5	5.6	5.4	8.5	7.6
Spanish Origin[a]												
Single	74.4	44.7	20.3	10.2	7.3	4.9						
Married, wife present	.20.1	44.7	63.1	67.4	67.4	68.2						
Separated	4.7	4.7	6.9	8.7	10.6	11.5						
Widowed	—	0.4	0.9	1.8	1.8	4.6						
Divorced	0.8	3.4	7.0	10.0	12.0	12.8						

[a]Persons of Spanish origin may be of any race.

Source: U.S. Bureau of the Census, "Marital Status and Family Status: March 1970," P-20, no. 212, Table 1; "Marital Status and Living Arrangements: March 1982," Current Population Reports, P-20, no. 380, Table 1.

were married. In both 1970 and 1982, most white and Spanish-origin women over age 25 were married. The differences can be noted in every marital status category: black women aged 25 to 44 are more likely to be single, separated, or divorced in every age group and, reflecting higher male mortality, at ages 35 to 44 black women are more likely to be widowed as well. A majority of black males over 30 are married (see Table 7.3). However, like black females, black males are more likely to be single, separated and divorced than either white or Spanish-origin males. The economic and demographic implications of these trends have been documented repeatedly (e.g., U.S. House of Representatives, Select Committee on Children, Youth and Families, 1983). We are more concerned with the origins of these trends and with their implications for teenagers' attitudes and goals.

Reasons for Differing Marriage Patterns

Cherlin (1981), noting that the historic pattern of earlier marriage among blacks has reversed since World War II, comments that "recent scholarship has rejected some conventional explanations, but scholars have not yet offered a satisfactory alternative" (Cherlin, 1981:100). Slavery, for example, and the migration of blacks to urban areas cannot explain changes recorded over the last decade. Cherlin suggests, in view of the high proportion of blacks not married, that "marriage seems to be less central to the family lives of a substantial segment of the black population than it is to Americans in general. For many blacks, ties to a network of kin may be the more important family bond over the long run" (Cherlin, 1981:110).

Is marriage less central to blacks than to other race or ethnic groups? Heiss (1981) notes that three perspectives on this question each have a following. First, some argue that blacks and whites accept equally the "mainstream family model." Second, it is argued that differences exist but they are due to socioeconomic status rather than race. Others argue, third, that blacks and whites hold different values regarding marriage. Heiss finds significant but modest racial differences in the centrality of marriage.

For the purposes of this study, we feel it is important to differentiate between values and attitudes, values being much more profound, personal and resistant to change, attitudes reflecting opinions, experience, and preferences. It is our view that value differences are slight, but attitudes differences are often substantial. However, we were able to find very little definitive evidence relevant to this question.

Marriage is highly valued in the general culture and in Judeo-Christian tradition, and there is good reason to suppose that blacks share in this general cultural value. One piece of evidence is that the overwhelming majority of young people intend to marry, regardless of race (see Table 7.4). Black youth are slightly more likely to plan to never marry; but only about one in twenty

TABLE 7.4
Age Respondents "Would Like to Marry," by Sex, Race, and Ethnicity, 1979

	Females			Males		
Age	White	Black	Hispanic	White	Black	Hispanic
Under 20	7.3	4.5	7.0	2.6	1.9	3.3
20 to 24	57.2	43.1	55.7	42.7	31.8	43.2
25 to 29	29.3	36.1	31.3	41.5	41.7	42.6
30 and Over	4.2	10.3	4.0	10.5	19.2	9.3
Never	2.1	6.0	1.9	3.1	5.3	1.6

Source: The Urban Institute, tabulations from the 1979 National Longitudinal Survey of Youth

TABLE 7.5
Importance of Marriage to Adults 18 to 49 Years of Age, by
Sex and Race, 1971

	Females		Males	
	White	Black	White	Black
	%	%	%	%
Most important[a]	48	15	34	19
Most or extremely important	84	56	74	65
Very important	12	26	19	17
Quite, somewhat, or not at all important	4	18	8 *	19
(N)	(620)	(84)	(481)	(54)

[a]Includes respondents who said that marriage is both extremely imporant and that marriage is one of the two most important domains of those listed.
Source: Willard Rodgers, special tabulation of the 1971 Quality of Life Survey, Survey Research Center, Institute for Social Research, University of Michigan.

blacks give this response. In addition, data from a special tabulation of the 1971 Quality of Life Survey, provided courtesy of Dr. Willard Rodgers at The University of Michigan, indicate that a majority of both black and white adults consider marriage to be extremely important to them and that very few adults rank marriage as not very important (see Table 7.5). However, it is also clear that a considerably higher proportion of whites, particularly white females, rank marriage as very important and as one of the two most important domains of those included in the Quality of Life Survey. Although sample sizes are somewhat small for black respondents, the differences by race are fairly substantial.

Other data indicate that black marriages are far more likely to be disrupted by divorce and separation than white marriages, even when social and economic factors are held constant (Moore and Waite, 1981) and that pregnant black teens are less likely to marry to resolve a pregnancy (O'Connell and Moore, 1980). Hatchet (1983) reports that black women rank economic factors higher than companionship as reasons for marriage. Black youth also prefer to be older when they marry, relative to whites and Hispanics. In addition, the desired age at first birth is earlier than the desired age at marriage for a substantial minority of blacks (see Tables 7.4, 7.8 and 7.9).

If black youth and adults share with other racial and ethnic groups a set of cultural values that support and encourage the notion of marriage, then what factors explain the lesser involvement of blacks with marriage?

Carlson (1979) and Kenkel (1981) note a number of reasons that marriage is less common among blacks. Economic factors rank high among factors. For one, high unemployment rates in the black community pose a barrier to establishing an economically viable marriage. Whether it is a young couple faced with a premarital pregnancy but lacking job prospects or a married couple faced with repeated spells of unemployment, not having earnings to rely on undercuts the ability of blacks to form and maintain marriages. Many families, of course, support young couples until they are able to become self-supporting. However, black families tend to have lower incomes and thus face greater difficulty in subsidizing young couples as they get started. The higher unemployment of young blacks may also mean that family support for a young couple must go on a longer time, intensifying the drain on family resources. In addition, the larger families of blacks mean that family resources must be stretched among more children, further depleting the assistance that parents might provide a young couple. Setting up a married household may also be more difficult for blacks because access to housing that is suitable or acceptable is more limited.

Black females are more oriented toward employment, and this may make them less disposed toward marriage (Kenkel, 1981), though White (1981) reports that marriages occur somewhat earlier for black women if their income is relatively high, the opposite of the income effect for whites. In general, black women seem more likely than white women to anticipate employment after marriage (Cherlin, 1980). Consequently, employment may serve more of a "dowry" function in the black community. If so, this implies that poor employment prospects for both males and females delay marriage in the black community.

The effect of welfare on marriage decisions is pertinent as well. As Moore and Burt note:

> The effects of welfare, if any, seem likely to differ at different decision points. Although it seems somewhat unlikely that the meager benefits available to welfare mothers would actually induce a young woman to become pregnant, it is possible that the availability of welfare support encourages a teenager, once she is pregnant, to bear a child when she might otherwise have obtained an abortion. Welfare may also make it possible for a woman to avoid marrying the father of her child if she has doubts about his stability or earning ability. . . . In addition, the availability of welfare may be a deciding factor in whether an unwed mother keeps her child or gives the child up for adoption. The attractiveness of the welfare option is affected, in theory, by the size of the welfare benefit, as well as by the attractiveness of the woman's alternatives, for example, the wage that she could earn in the labor market (Moore and Burt, 1982:109–110).

For significant numbers of people at the bottom of the economic ladder, the stability of welfare as a source of income and the fact that eligibility for AFDC (Aid to Families with Dependent Children) automatically results in eligibility for Medicaid must mean that AFDC compares favorably with the income, job security, and fringe benefits available from employment. Empirical studies of this issue have been few and inconclusive (see Moore and Burt, 1982, for review). The difficulty in evaluating the impact of welfare lies in the fact that both AFDC and Medicaid are available to all babies born outside of marriage; thus the independent variable is a constant. Researchers have explored the effect of varied benefit levels on fertility; but further work should explore the relative income that can be obtained from welfare compared to employment of the woman and/or a prospective husband. The level of earnings, income stability, and the level of associated fringe benefits all need to be considered. Some proportion of couples for whom welfare income exceeds earned income probably choose welfare over marriage; but the frequency of such a pattern is unknown and specific factors leading to choosing welfare over work are not understood.

Carlson (1979) suggests that the relatively great availability of kin among blacks also provides a substitute for marriage. Several studies do indicate that pregnant black teenagers are more likely to receive support from their families than white teen mothers (Williams, 1977; Miller, 1983). Hofferth (1982) also finds that black single parents received more assistance from kin. Stack (1974) describes an assistance network among low-income urban blacks that helps to cushion individuals from the vicissitudes of life in poverty. Relying on this network seemed for many in the community she studied to be safer than relying on a marriage. However, white teens also have families, and their families tend to have greater resources in absolute terms. Thus it seems unlikely that black teens have out-of-wedlock births simply because they have kin they can rely on rather than a husband. On the other hand, black families seem to be more helpful to young mothers, and it may be that this undermines teen fears of becoming a mother (Johnson, 1983). One cannot argue cause versus effect on the basis of current research, though. Reliance on kin among blacks may be as much or more a function of not being married as a factor in the decision not to marry.

The ratio of males to females in the population may also affect the likelihood of marriage. Guttentag and Secord (1983) stress the importance of unequal numbers of black males and females on patterns of marriage and divorce among U.S. blacks. In their words,

> Suppose there were more young adult women than men. Under those circumstances, many of the women would not be able to find a man to marry and would have difficulty finding casual partners. How would this affect the birth rate in a population? How would this make women feel? What kinds of actions might they take? Would their attitudes and behaviors toward men change? Would they begin to relate differently toward other women? Would women get together in protest? Would they want to become less dependent on men?

> And what about the men? With an unusual number of women available, what would they do? Would their attitudes and behaviors toward women change? In what way? Would they be more promiscuous? What about men who were already married? Would a surplus of single women have any effects on their marriages? Would the presence of available single women influence a husband's attitude toward his wife? Would it be easier for him to have an affair? Would the temptations be greater? Under what circumstances, if at all? Would the persistence of this imbalanced sex ratio ultimately bring about the profound changes in the relationship between men and women and in the nature of the family? (Guttentag and Secord, 1983:13-14).

Guttentag and Secord argue strongly that the critical factor affecting the balance of power and dependency in a relationship is the level of alternatives each person has in the form of other relationships. Obviously other chacteristics such as personality and values are pertinent to one's level of alternatives and to the satisfactions a person provides or receives in a relationship. Whatever the source of satisfaction, though, it is assumed within social exchange theory that individuals will attempt to maximize their own satisfaction outcomes. This implies that people will choose the most satisfying relationship, if they have a choice.

Without necessarily being fully conscious or calculating, a process of negotiating and bargaining is argued to occur in a relationship. "When one sex is in short supply, all relationships between opposite-sexed persons are potentially affected in a similar way. The individual member whose sex is in short supply has a stronger position and is less dependent on the partner because of the larger number of alternative relationships available'' (Guttentag and Secord, 1983:23). This imbalance is expected to lead men to be reluctant to make and maintain a commitment to a wife and family, producing relatively high rates of out-of-wedlock fertility and divorce. Women are expected to experience more stress and anger, to develop more negative attitudes about marriage; yet they might also respond to their poorer bargaining position by giving in more to male demands.

Are black males in relatively short supply? Underenumeration of young minority males represents a problem in assessing this situation. As shown in Table 7.6, the sex ratio is lower for blacks than for whites at every age, due to higher mortality among black males, but probably to underenumeration as well.

Guttentag and Secord present data based on the 1970 Census on the number of unmarried black males by age compared to the number of unmarried females two years younger (see Figure 7.1). These data illustrate a dramatic shortage of black males. Much of the shortfall is probably a product of underenumeration. However, the absolute number of persons is not really the most relevant factor anyhow. Difficult as it is to assess, the number of marriageable men relative to the number of marriageable women is the crucial issue.

Black men are substantially more likely to be institutionalized than black women or white men (see Table 7.7). In 1970, just among men 20 to 24, 4.7 percent of black males were counted in the Census as being in some kind of institution, primarily correctional institutions, compared to 1.1 percent of white males. (Preliminary data from the 1980 Census suggest a continuation of this discrepancy.) If the number of men without employment were added in, assuming that men without earnings are not very marriageable, the higher

TABLE 7.6
Sex Ratio (number of males per 100 females), by Race, 1981

Age	All Races	Whites	Blacks
All ages	94.5	95.2	89.7
Under 14	104.5	105.3	101.6
14 to 24	102.3	103.1	97.0
25 to 44	97.7	99.6	85.7
45 to 64	90.7	91.9	80.4
65 and Over	67.3	67.0	67.2

Source: U.S. Bureau of the Census, "Statistical Abstract of the United States, 1982–83." Washington, D.C.: U.S. Government Printing Office, Table 29.

FIGURE 7.1
Marital Opportunities of Black Women, by Age, from 1960 to 1990

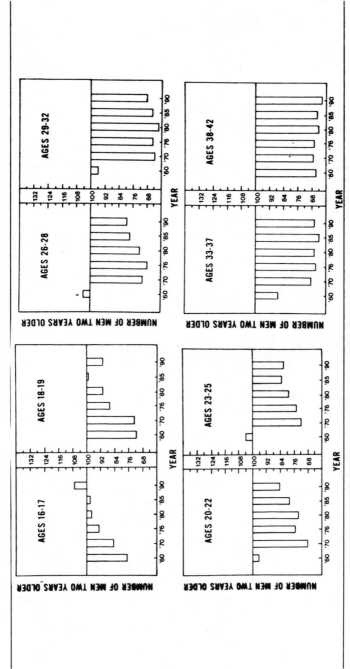

Source: U.S Bureau of the Census, *Census of the Population: 1960, Subject Reports, Marital Status,* Final Report PC(2)-4C, Table 1; *Census of the Population: 1970, Subject Reports, Marital Status,* Final Report PC(2)-4C, Table 1: *Current Population Reports, Projections of the Population of the United States: 1977 to 2050,* Series P-25, No. 704. Washington, DC: Government Printing Office. Taken from Guttentag and Secord, *Too Many Women,* 1983.

TABLE 7.7
Institutionalization Rates per 100,000 Persons Ages 20–24, by
Type of Institution

| | (Males per 100,000 Population) | | | |
| | White | | Nonwhite | |
	1950	1970	1950	1970
All types of institutions	1,111	1,117	3,750	4,749
Mental	186	180	426	422
Aged and Dependent	11	23	24	30
Correctional	647	665	2,991	3,865
Mentally Handicapped	174	189	87	184
Tuberculosis	54	3	139	9
All Other	39	57	83	239

| | (Females per 100,000 Population) | | | |
| | White | | Nonwhite | |
	1950	1970	1950	1970
All types of institutions	395	274	640	458
Mental	106	81	185	134
Aged and Dependent	13	17	9	6
Correctional	26	25	185	171
Mentally Handicapped	156	126	73	109
Tuberculosis	67	2	156	14
All Other	27	23	32	24

Source: "Task Panel Reports Submitted to the Presidential Commission on Mental Health,"
   vol 11, Appendix, Table 15.

unemployment rates of black males would exacerbate the imbalance. Black
males are also less likely to have jobs that pay well and provide fringe benefits,
such as medical care. Women may not consider men with poorly paid jobs
that lack health insurance as good marriage prospects.

Persuasive as this theory is, we know of no research evaluating whether
and to what extent these kinds of factors affect the marriage decisions of
women and men, black or white. In addition, since the absolute numbers of
males and females are most nearly equal during the teen years, when the
proportion of out-of-wedlock births is the highest, the sex ratio argument
cannot be applied in a simple, straightforward manner to the issue of teenage
fertility. However, the difficulties experienced by older blacks in establishing
and maintaining marriages may be salient to teens. Teens may observe that
adults hold values toward marriage and family life that they are not able to

fulfill. Do adult difficulties affect the attitudes that black teenagers hold regarding marriage?

Attitudes Toward Marriage

We have not been able to locate studies linking family background characteristics with teenager's attitudes toward marriage, or studies linking community characteristics with these attitudes. Yet there is no reason to assume that causality runs from negative attitudes toward marriage to lower wages, higher unemployment, and an imbalanced sex ratio. Therefore, we assume that, if there is a causal relationship, it is that the social and economic realities of black marriage patterns have affected the attitudes of black youth toward marriage. And black youth do seem to hold different attitudes toward marriage and family formation than white youth.

Data from the National Longitudinal Survey of Youth shown above (see Table 7.4) indicate that blacks, both female and male, are less likely to want to marry before the age of 20 than white or Hispanic youth. Unfortunately, the interview question was precoded into age categories, precluding more detailed comparisons.

Data from a special tabulation of the 1981 National Survey of Children, courtesy of Dr. James Peterson of Child Trends, Inc., are presented in Tables 7.8 and 7.9. The top panel of Table 7.8 indicates the proportion of girls and boys aged 11-16 who would like to marry before particular ages. Again a higher proportion of white girls prefer early marriage, and black males are particularly unlikely to favor early marriage. In fact, nearly half of the black males indicated they would prefer to be 25 or older at first marriage, compared to 30 percent of the white males. Interesting as the racial differences are, however, it should be noted that few respondents of either race or sex in either the National Longitudinal Survey of Youth or the National Survey of Children preferred to be less than 20 when they first married.

Data from the National Survey of Children presented in the lower panel of Table 7.8 provide a startling contrast to the data in the top panel. Regarding the age at which the youths would prefer to have their first child, blacks, both male and female, indicate a younger age than whites. In fact, greater proportions of blacks prefer to have a child during their teen years than prefer to marry during their teens. These data are summarized in Table 7.9. Among black girls, 10.7 percent prefer to marry before the age of 20, while 22.2 percent would like to have a child before turning 20. Among black males, the figures are 3.7 percent who favor early marriage and 15.4 percent who favor early parenting for themselves. Among whites, both males and females, higher proportions prefer to marry than to have a child during their teen years. Again, it should be noted that large proportions of all groups prefer to delay

TABLE 7.8
Preferred Age at First Marriage and First Birth, Children 11–16, 1981

| | Age at Which Respondents Would Like to Marry | | | |
| | Females | | Males | |
	Whites	Blacks	Whites	Blacks
19 and under	13.4	10.7	7.1	3.7
20	24.0	20.2	16.8	11.8
21	12.8	18.1	18.1	18.2
22	10.1	6.1	10.6	6.5
23	9.2	6.1	7.4	3.4
24	8.1	10.8	7.4	3.9
25 and Over	20.5	27.6	29.9	49.0
Not marry	1.2	0.5	1.2	3.4

| | Age at Which Respondents Would Like to Have a First Child | | | |
| | Females | | Males | |
	Whites	Blacks	Whites	Blacks
19 and under	5.7	22.2	5.8	15.4
20	14.2	12.9	6.1	10.6
21	8.1	13.9	7.2	10.7
22	7.3	6.8	8.1	4.8
23	10.6	8.2	8.0	4.0
24	10.6	6.7	8.7	7.3
25 and over	41.7	28.4	54.1	45.4
Never	0.8	0.9	1.5	2.1

Source: James Peterson, Child Trends, Inc., special tabulation of data from the 1981 National Survey of Children.

having their first child and that there is considerable variation regarding these preferences among blacks and whites.

Data from a study of male, low-income, black students attending junior high school in Baltimore (Clark, Zabin, and Hardy, 1984) indicate a similar tendency for childbearing to be preferred at a younger age than marriage (see Table 7.10). Although the average age preferred for a first birth is 21 for girls, it can be assumed that a substantial proportion gave an ideal age lower than 20 to produce a mean of 21. As interesting as the lower preferred age for childbearing relative to marriage is, one should also note, the very low preferred age for beginning to have intercourse. Youth who begin to have sex at 15 and who want a first birth in their early twenties face six or seven years of what must be highly effective contraception if they are to realize their intentions. Data abound indicating that many fail to avoid pregnancy for this length of time. One thing we don't know is whether junior high

TABLE 7.9
Percent Preferring to Have First Child or Enter First Marriage before the Age of 20, by Race and Sex

| | Females Age 15 - 19[a] | | | |
| | 1971 | | 1976 | |
	Whites	Blacks	Whites	Blacks
Ideal age to have first baby is less than 20	5.2	34.1	6.5	35.2

| | 1981[b] | | | |
| | Females Age 11 to 16 | | Males Age 11 to 16 | |
	Whites	Blacks	Whites	Blacks
Age like to have first birth is less than 20	5.7	22.2	5.8	15.4
Age like to marry is less than 20	13.4	10.7	7.1	3.7

Sources: [a]National Survey of Young Women, in Zelnik, M., J. Kantner and K. Ford, *Sex and Pregnancy in Adolescence* (Beverly Hills: Sage, 1981), Table 2.18.
[b]James Peterson, Child Trends, Inc., "National Survey of Children," 1983, special tabulation.

students think they can have sex and still postpone pregnancy for six or seven years. Do they regard their aspirations as reasonable? To what extent do these ideals affect teen behavior?

While the attitudes of a young person 11 to 16 may not predict the age at which he or she actually marries or has a first child, the fact that a substantial proportion of blacks express a preference for earlier childbearing than marriage may suggest that there is greater acceptability for early, out-of-wedlock childbearing among some black youth. Data from the National Survey of Young Women in both 1971 and 1976 also indicate that a substantial minority of black females aged 15 to 19 prefer to have their first child during their teen years. Regrettably, Professors Zelnik and Kantner have not published data they collected on desired age at first marriage by race; however, other data from their surveys are relevant here.

As shown in Table 7.11, the majority of black and white females feel that society at large condemns an unwed mother. However, black teens are far less likely to perceive strong condemnation in their own neighborhoods than

TABLE 7.10
Ideal Age at First Intercourse, First Birth, and First Marriage for Males and Females, among a Sample of Black Junior and Senior High Males

	Males	Females
Ideal age at first intercourse	16.1	16.2
Ideal age at first birth	22.5	21.8
Ideal age at first marriage	24.5	23.6

Source: S. Clark, L. Zabin, and J. Hardy, "Sex, Contraception and Parenthood: Experience and Attitudes among Urban Black Young Men," *Family Planning Perspectives* 16(1984): 77–82.

TABLE 7.11
Perception of Condemnation of an Unwed Mother by Society and by Neighborhood, Females Ages 15–19 in 1976, by Race

	Perception of Societal Condemnation		Perception of Neighborhood Condemnation	
	Whites	Blacks	Whites	Blacks
Very strongly	18.9	23.1	31.2	17.7
Strongly	36.3	29.7	27.6	18.6
Somewhat	38.8	30.6	28.5	26.4
Not at all	4.8	13.6	10.1	32.7

Source: M. Zelnik, John Kantner, and K. Ford, *Sex and Pregnancy in Adolescence* (Beverly Hills: Sage, 1981), Tables 2.11, 2.12.

are white teens. These data parallel reports from several research studies that black teen mothers anticipate less disapproval from peers. Williams (1977), for example, reports that 70 percent of the pregnant black girls in his sample anticipated a favorable reaction from peers and 65 percent expected a favorable response from the baby's father. Forty percent and 43 percent, respectively, of the pregnant white teens in this Rochester, New York, sample held similarly positive expectations. Parental reactions were expected to be negative among both whites and blacks, however, and they were in fact negative. In general, though, blacks seem to hold more tolerant attitudes toward early and out-of-wedlock childbearing. While these attitudes may be very positive in some ways—showing acceptance and support for the mother and a caring concern for the baby—the presence of a greater degree of tolerance may undermine an important historical barrier to early, nonmarital fertility, that of social disapproval.

As white attitudes toward childbearing outside of marriage have become more liberal (Zelnik et al., 1981), the out-of-wedlock birth rate among young whites has risen as well. Empirical data establishing a causal link do not exist, and it may be that attitudes soften as a practice becomes more common, as well as the reverse. In addition, the preventive value of social disapproval, if documented, would need to be weighed against any costs to the mother and baby of such social disapproval. For example, greater disapproval may lead to more abortion, more forced marriage, or more rejection of mother and baby by those who could help them, rather than leading to fewer out-of-wedlock pregnancies. Alternatively, perhaps a different sort of negative attitude could be substituted, one that doesn't condemn the baby or mother but acknowledges that early and unwed parenthood is difficult economically and psychologically and is therefore to be avoided. This attitude may already be fairly common, actually, and sex education programs that bring home the consequences of teenage childbearing to students may be helping to spread such an attitude. At present, however, ample evidence exists that while blacks do not value early marriage, there is greater tolerance in the black community for early and nonmarital fertility. While data do not exist indicating that such tolerance causes teenage pregnancy, it can be assumed that tolerant attitudes do not discourage early childbearing. Thus we conclude that greater tolerance of nonmarital childbearing among blacks may be a factor in the higher fertility rates of black teenagers. Such attitudes arise, we think, from the difficulties blacks in the United States have had in establishing and maintaining stable marriages. The effect of black marriage patterns on teenage fertility is not limited to the possible impact on attitudes, however.

One-Parent Homes and Teenage Parenthood

Black children are considerably more likely to grow up in single-parent homes. In 1982, only 42 percent of black children under age 18 were living with two parents, compared to 69 percent of Spanish origin children and 81 percent of white children (U.S. Bureau of the Census, 1983, Table E). Nearly half of all black children live with their mother only. Given the poverty of black single-parent families, this means that black children are growing up in lower income homes in lower income neighborhoods. They have only one parent in the home to supervise them. In addition, the dating of their unmarried parent may provide a model for nonmarital sexual relationships. These same factors may be important in single-parent homes regardless of race or ethnicity;

but the higher incidence of black children growing up in single-parent homes means that any such influences affect a larger proportion of black children.

Numerous studies have documented that girls from single-parent homes are more likely to become mothers at a young age. Using data from the National Longitudinal Survey of Young Women in a three-stage least squares model of early family formation, Moore and Hofferth (1980) found that girls who did not live with both natural parents at age 14 were significantly more likely to have an early birth. The relationship was found among both blacks and whites and was slightly larger for blacks. Freeman et al. (1982) found that among black family planning clinic patients, teens from one-parent households were more likely to have become pregnant within 12 months of the first interview. Devaney and Hubley (1981) using the 1971 National Survey of Young Women found only nonsignificant effects of family structure. However, Hogan and Kitagawa (1983) found family structure to be an important factor among black teenage females in Chicago. Teens from non-intact families were found to be 34 percent more likely to be sexually experienced and 52 percent more likely to have been pregnant, net of numerous other factors.

Data collected in 1976 in the second National Survey of Young Women clearly show an association between family structure and teenagers' attitudes toward sexual activity and their degree of sexual experience (see Table 7-12, Panel A). Teenagers from "ideal"[1] family backgrounds are considerably less likely to feel that premarital intercourse is always all right and less likely to have had premarital intercourse themselves. These differences are stronger among whites; but black teens from stable two-parent homes are also considerably less likely to have had coitus and tend to be somewhat less tolerant toward premarital sex as well. Data from the National Survey of Children show a similar pattern for blacks and for white females (see Panel B of Table 7.12). Race differences exist despite family structure; but, with the interesting exception of white males, teens from nonintact families are more likely to have initiated sex by age 15 to 16 than teens reared in a two-parent home. Thornton (1983) reports similar results for a sample of whites in Detroit.

What is it about being raised in a single-parent home that might lead to a higher incidence of early childbearing? The most distinctive characteristic of single-parent families is their poverty. Having a low income has a variety of effects on families, ranging from obvious economic effects to interpersonal effects.

The effect of income as it translates into neighborhood quality may be important, to judge from the Hogan and Kitagawa study. Controlling for numerous family and individual level variables, they found that black adolescents growing up in a poverty area of Chicago had a probability of having had intercourse that was 90 percent higher than comparable black teens growing up in another Chicago neighborhood. The probability of pregnancy was

TABLE 7.12

Attitudes Toward Premarital Sex and Percentage Reporting Premarital Sex by
Family Type and Race, Among Females 15 to 19 in 1976, (Panel A); and
Percentage Reporting Sexual Experience Among Youth 15 to 16 in 1981, by
Presence of Father, Race, and Sex (Panel B)

PANEL A--Attitudes Toward and Percentage Reporting Premarital Sex

	Sex Always All Right	All Right if Planning to Marry	Never All Right	Percentage Reporting Premarital Intercourse
White Females **15 to 19**				
Ideal[a]	18.9	35.2	45.9 = 100%	32.2
Less Ideal	30.6	37.2	32.2 = 100%	48.0
Least Ideal	30.5	39.4	30.1 = 100%	51.8
Black Females **15 to 19**				
Ideal	45.2	28.2	26.6 = 100%	52.3
Less Ideal	50.9	30.3	18.8 = 100%	73.3
Least Ideal	52.9	25.5	21.7 = 100%	69.5

PANEL B--Percentage Reporting Sexual Experience

	Black Males Percent (n)		Black Females Percent (n)		White Males Percent (n)		White Females Percent (n)	
No father in home	42.0	(28)	31.3	(37)	12.3	(29)	24.9	(28)
Biological or adoptive father father in home	30.6	(19)	14.6	(13)	22.6	(122)	9.1	(132)
Other father, father substitute in home	[62.1]	(5)	71.3	(9)	13.1	(21)	52.9	(14)

[a]Girls raised in families termed "ideal" were raised by both their natural or adoptive mother and father for at least their first 15 years. Girls in the "least ideal" category were raised by a single parent, in a foster home, or by a family surrogate. The "less ideal" category meets most but not all of the conditions for the ideal situation.

Source: Panel A: M. Zelnik, J. Kantner, and K. Ford, *Sex and Pregnancy in Adolescence* (Beverly Hills: Sage, 1981), Tables 2.10, 3.2; Panel B: James Peterson, Child Trends, Inc., "National Survey of Children," unpublished tabulation.

estimated to be 42 percent higher at each age for the blacks living in the poverty neighborhood. Moore, Peterson, and Furstenberg (1984) also found that 15- and 16-year-olds living in an "excellent" or "very good" neighborhood were less likely to have initiated sexual activity, net of family structure, the youth's educational aspirations, and the parents' educational level.

In fact, among black females, controlling for parent education and race accounted for nearly all of the effect of family structure. In the other subgroups and in the Chicago study, the neighborhood effect occurred in addition to the effect of family structure noted above. Thus, while children raised by single parents may suffer neighborhood disadvantages, this does not seem to explain the entire effect of the single-parent family or the effect among all subgroups.

Supervision as it relates to teenage fertility is not a factor that has been much studied. Moore, Peterson, and Furstenberg (1984) found little evidence that overall supervision relates to early sexual activity. As they note, high supervision may be a response to poor behavior as often as it is a cause of good behavior. Supervision of early dating behavior per se was studied by Hogan and Kitagawa (1983). They find that supervision affects rates of intercourse and pregnancy. Black females whose early dating experiences were closely supervised by their parents were found to have a probability of intercourse only 55 percent as high as those not so closely supervised and to have a possibility of pregnancy only 57 percent as high, net of other variables in their model.

Students in our school interviews also seemed to find the number of parents in the home to be pertinent information. For example, they seemed to pick up on the fact that the Sandra/Joe story stem describes a one-parent situation. One girl commented, "Without a father, there's not as good training." Another girl felt this didn't make a difference but a third felt that with her father gone and her mother working, "Sandra didn't have a relationship with her mother." Later, discussing Mary, whose father was depicted as a lawyer, the advantages of having two parents came up. One girl commented that Mary's parents can afford college, and another added that "Getting pregnant would ruin everything she's gotten going." "Having two parents doesn't mean she talked with them," another girl commented, "but she would think about them—a good relationship. She wouldn't want to hurt them." Thus certain advantages, both economic and nonmaterial, were attributed to two-parent families, spontaneously if not inevitably, by the students.

Charles Ballard, a community worker in Cleveland who has focused on teen fathers, feels that the kids he works with are profoundly affected by the absence of their fathers (Ballard, 1983). In his community, he reports, the teens often don't know who their father is or where he is. They feel angry, hurt, and unimportant due to what they perceive as parental unconcern and disinterest. This can lead to pregnancy he argues, out of a desire on the part of the teen to be important and to be loved. While teens from two-parent families can well have such feelings as well, Ballard thinks the problem is more acute when fathers are absent, especially when contact with the absent father is virtually nonexistent. The validity and significance of such impressions are difficult to document; however, analyses of the 1981 National Survey of Children support Ballard's impressions. Children in one-parent families were substantially less likely to report feeling close to both parents or to either parent. Moreover, children close to neither parent were particularly likely to be described by parents as depressed and withdrawn, as exhibiting antisocial behavior and as having behavior problems at school (Peterson and Zill, 1983). The relative neglect of this topic argues for further research.

Another difference between one-parent and two-parent households is that single parents are likely to be dating, while married couples presumably are not dating or having partners to the home. Moore, Peterson, and Furstenberg (1984) found that white daughters of nonmarried mothers were more likely to be sexually active if the mother was dating frequently than if she did not date very much. Sample sizes were small, however, and the association did not hold for black daughters. Thus the question of whether and how parents' social lives might affect teenage behavior requires considerably more study. If the mother or father is obviously having a sexual relationship though unmarried, does the teenager accept this as a model for his or her own behavior?

It would appear from research to date that the association between being raised by one parent and becoming pregnant as an adolescent is not simple or straightforward, nor does the meaning of family structure seem to be the same for blacks and whites or males and females. There appear to be multiple sources of risk that are related to having but one parent, and these are both economic and social. The impact of these risks may be additive, but it seems likely that it is multiplicative. That is, poverty and a lack of supervision, for example, may interact in ways that exacerbate the risk of early parenthood beyond any risk implied by these factors separately. At present, however, the link between teen pregnancy and growing up in a single-parent family has not been definitively explained. It would be helpful to have a better understanding of the underlying process, since such an understanding might reveal intervention points that are more amenable to change than is the marital status of the parent generation.

Conclusions

Large differences exist between black and white marriage patterns. Less strong but still significant differences can be noted between the attitudes of blacks and whites about marriage. Most black youth expect to marry eventually, but a significant minority prefer to delay marriage past the age when they want to have their first child. In addition, black youth perceive their neighborhoods to be more tolerant of out-of-wedlock childbearing and they themselves are considerably more tolerant of early, nonmarital sex. Many factors in the social and economic position of blacks in the United States can be noted as the cause of such differences, particularly the lower earnings and more frequent unemployment in the black community and the lower ratio of black males to females. However, our concern must be with the implications of such differences.

Black children growing up today are considerably less likely to enjoy the advantages of having two parents—particularly the higher income and better neighborhoods enjoyed by children in two-parent households. Other differences may include less supervision, less attention from the parent(s), and the example of parental dating in one-parent homes; however, evidence that these factors affect teenage pregnancy is only beginning to accumulate and a causal link with family structure has not been established. We suggest that further research be done from the perspective of looking at the successes.

Many low-income and particularly minority families are strained and stretched to the point that they cannot meet the challenges posed by their neighborhoods. Youth in many low-income neighborhoods are confronted with few examples of adults who are engaged in steady legitimate work and who are maintaining stable two-parent families. In addition, they are provided with few opportunities to accomplish and move ahead via legitimate activities. On the other hand, youth are presented with many examples of illicit employment, early sexual activity, and erratic family life. Raising a child in such a setting is a formidable task. Those who succeed have succeeded against all odds, and it is these successes that should be studied. Failure is not surprising; it is almost ensured by the environment. Yet failure is not inevitable. Children that grow up on the same floor of a public housing project do turn out differently.

What characteristics of family structure, attitudes, work patterns, community involvement, religious belief, intellectual ability, athletic talent, or family cohesion differentiate those families that are able to protect or insulate their children from environments that would overwhelm most people? This is, of course, a variant of a very general and age-old question about what makes a good parent; but it is not the same old question. It takes for granted that, while parenting is a challenge to all parents, some families face greater difficulties than others. It acknowledges that parents rearing children without adequate resources face great difficulty in ensuring abstinence or in fostering effective contraception and assumes that those who succeed nevertheless must have some special attributes or resources that elevate their probabilities of success above what might otherwise be expected. Since the economic and social constraints that encumber black families are unlikely to disappear overnight, it seems important to examine those factors in the family and the community that enhance the functioning of black families and to build on them.

Note

1. Girls raised in families termed "ideal" were raised by both their natural or adoptive mother and father for at least their first 15 years. Girls in the "least ideal" category were raised by a single parent, in a foster home, or by a parent surrogate. The "less ideal" category meets most but not all of the conditions for the "ideal" situation.

8

Summary and Conclusions

Summary of Chapters One through Seven

Teenage Childbearing

By the time they turn 18, more than a quarter of young black women are already mothers, compared to less than ten percent of whites. More than four in ten contemporary black women have a child by the time they turn 20, compared to two in ten young white women. Although the number of births to black teens has fallen over the past decade, as has the fertility rate (births per 1,000 females), black teenagers in the United States still have much higher fertility rates than teenagers in any other developed nation. Not only are fertility rates far higher among black teens, but births to blacks are substantially more likely to occur outside of marriage. Among teens aged 18 to 19, the out-of-wedlock birth rate is more than four times higher among blacks than among whites. Among teens aged 15 to 17, it is more than five times higher.

In a purely descriptive sense, these differences arise because black teenagers are considerably more likely to begin having sexual intercourse at an early age (see Tables 2.11 and 2.12) and, among those sexually active, blacks are more likely to become pregnant (see Tables 2.14 and 2.15). Although the proportion of all pregnancies ending in abortion is similar for blacks and whites, because of their higher incidence of pregnancy, blacks of all ages have a higher abortion rate than whites. Black teens have an abortion rate twice that of white teens, but even this high reliance on abortion has not reduced their fertility rate to the level of white teens.

Black teens who carry to term are also considerably less likely to marry before their child is born compared to whites, and they seldom relinquish their babies for adoption. These striking differences in the fertility behavior of black and white teens, further described in chapter 2, "A Review of Fertility Data," are the starting point for this study.

A Model for Exploring Teenage Sexual Behavior

Given accumulating evidence that early childbearing has important social and economic implications for young mothers and their families and for society at large (see Moore and Burt, 1982), the disproportionate incidence of teenage motherhood in the black community is a source of concern. To address this issue, we have chosen to focus on the factors that motivate teenagers to delay having sex or becoming pregnant.

"Why Don't Teens Become Pregnant?" As noted in chapter 1, this is the reverse of the question usually asked; but we feel this is appropriate because pregnancy occurs differently than most other achievements. Most often, it is necessary to work toward a goal. In the instance of pregnancy, the opposite tends to be true. Pregnancy occurs (for most couples) in the absence of effort. That is, it is typically necessary to expend some effort in order to avoid pregnancy, either by abstaining from sex or by diligently practicing contraception. From this perspective, we ask "what kinds of factors might be important in motivating teens to delay sex or pregnancy?" In this report, we have explored the role of educational aspirations and failure to complete high school; career aspirations and opportunity; and marriage expectations and attitudes as possible sources of such motivation.

The role that we envision for these motivating factors is that they provide the incentive many teenagers require if they are to resist the pressure of their peers, obtain information about sex and contraception, locate contraceptive services, and use birth control methods correctly and consistently. If motivation is low, we hypothesize, then even modest barriers to the acquisition of services or information may mean that the teenager does not obtain the knowledge or birth control methods necessary to avoid pregnancy, or the teenager may fail to use the knowledge or methods that are readily available. Thus, along with motivation, we also view the role of information and services as crucial. In the absence of an understanding of how pregnancy occurs or how pregnancy might be prevented, even highly motivated teenagers may not be able to avoid pregnancy. Similarly, if it is difficult to obtain birth control methods, then only those teens with the greatest motivation are expected to overcome the barriers to services. Throughout our review of the literature on these issues, we have been most concerned about racial differences in motivation, information, and access to services, since our primary interest lies in explaining the very large racial differences in the incidence of adolescent pregnancy. However, we have distinguished socioeconomic factors from racial factors wherever possible.

Information and Attitudes

Chapter 3 explores "Information and Attitudes" related to adolescent pregnancy. We find little indication that teenagers, even very young teenagers, are unaware of the basic facts of conception. In addition, few are unaware of the existence of ways to prevent pregnancy. However, complete and accurate information seem to be in short supply, particularly among blacks, among males, and among youth from families of lower socioeconomic status. Many teens do not perceive themselves to be at risk of pregnancy because they believe they are "too young," or they believe that "it can't happen to me." Some teens perceive birth control to be dangerous. In addition, many teens seem to lack crucial information regarding how to use a birth control method correctly. The absence of such information may serve as a cap on the effectiveness of adolescent efforts to avoid parenthood.

Sex education has been found to increase the information of teens and the probability of pregnancy is lower among students who have had sex education. Given evidence of significant information deficits, a need for earlier and more complete sex education seems clear. Many people are concerned, though, that providing sex education will encourage youths to have sex. Studies have found, however, that while sex education increases knowledge and leads to greater tolerance among students for the beliefs and behaviors of others, it does not affect students' own values or increase the incidence of premarital sex. That sex education can have any identifiable effect at all seems surprising, given the competing sources of information, often misinformation, to which teens are exposed, particularly from peers and the media.

As noted, there is some evidence indicating that black youth have less information about pregnancy and birth control. Other evidence indicates that black teens hold different attitudes toward sexual activity and pregnancy. More black teens favor having a birth before the age of 20, fewer blacks perceive community condemnation for out-of-wedlock childbearing, and more black teens anticipate a positive response to pregnancy from peers, though not from parents. These findings suggest that sex education that covers more than just reproductive physiology may be necessary to reduce the incidence of early pregnancy among black teens. It is important not to over-emphasize the racial differences, however. The need for better information is very great among both black and white teens. Programs for black teens may need to deal directly, though, with a somewhat different set of issues, for example, countering teens' perception that early and out-of-wedlock motherhood are relatively acceptable.

Another issue of particular concern for blacks (and increasingly for whites) is the need to reach youth at an early age. Forty-one percent of black females have already had sex by the time they are fifteen, compared to 18 percent of white females. Many school programs, and parents as well, do not provide in-depth sex education until teens are older (if ever). It may be difficult, however, to implement and even to design programs for this young age group. Sex and contraception are complex and emotional issues even for adults. The task of designing a sex education curriculum for youth who are not cognitively mature, who lack experience in life, and who are negotiating a variety of adolescent transitions is extremely difficult.

We are not sanguine about the possibilities of turning 13- and 14-year-olds into well-informed and efficient contraceptors for their initial sexual experiences. It is our considered opinion that most youths in their early teens and many youths in their middle and late teens are too young to handle contraception effectively. Other negative consequences of too-early sexual intercourse are also possible, but are similarly under-researched. Further research should be conducted to test these possibilities, we feel, since studies do not currently exist indicating at what age or ages teens become sufficiently mature both cognitively and emotionally to handle intense intimacy in a positive way and to manage the demanding task of contraception. If such research does establish that some age or age range is too young, then strong efforts should be initiated to encourage teens to delay sexual activity past that age.

In general there is much dispute in this society regarding when youth are old enough to be allowed to engage in behaviors viewed as "adult," for example drinking, voting, driving, living away from parents, etc. Questions of individual choice versus family and societal responsibility are at issue. While difficult questions are involved, these are good topics for sex education to address. Students might benefit greatly from debating the issues. Numerous evaluation studies have made it clear that sex education that provides merely the physiological facts is insufficient.

Sex education curricula need to help youth understand cause-effect processes, to appreciate the impact on them of their peers and the media, to articulate their personal goals and understand how parenthood might affect achievement of these goals, and to develop rational decision-making skills. Development of such skills should be useful to youth in general, in addition to helping youth delay pregnancy. Values clarification and training in communication also seem to be important components of effective sex education. In addition, coverage of controversial topics such as how to use contraceptive methods and where to obtain them seems necessary, given the effect such informational gaps can have on teenagers' attempts to prevent pregnancy.

Difficult as it may be to implement full-fledged sex education classes in the schools, we recommend that the schools, as well as parents and other community institutions, provide sex education. Studies to date consistently indicate that parents have not been able or willing to provide complete and accurate sex education to their children. Community institutions have developed excellent and innovative programs, but since participation is voluntary many of those youths most in need of better information will not be served unless such programs can be provided in the schools.

To summarize, the data make it clear that better information is needed by young people of all races, both male and female, and that additional information may be particularly helpful in reducing the high out-of-wedlock birth rate among black teenagers and teenagers from families of low socioeconomic status. The absence of such information can place a cap on the ability of youths to control their lives and achieve their goals. Also, as noted repeatedly, we strongly recommend wider dissemination of courses that provide not simply information but training in decision making and life planning. Even broad dissemination of such curricula should not be viewed as a panacea, however. The roles of teenagers' aspirations and service availability also require attention.

Contraception and Abortion

In chapter 4, "Contraception and Abortion," we estimate that about half of black and white teens at risk of pregnancy receive medical family planning services. Blacks are more likely to be served by organized family planning clinics, while whites are more likely to see a private physician; but about half of each group are served. Another perspective, of course, is that only half are served, and we must conclude that this proportion is much too low.

As a factor in explaining the higher fertility of blacks, however, it does not seem that clinic availability is the crucial factor. Whites are not more likely overall to have services available to them. In fact, since clinics are more often available in urban areas and services are often provided on a sliding scale, clinic services may be more available to low-income, urban black youth. In addition, since clinics typically serve all those patients who seek services, the supply of services can expand (to a point) if the demand expands. Consequently, other issues of accessibility and demand seem more central. Factors affecting accessibility include location, cost, hours of operation, and confidentiality of services. Results from one study suggest that white teens care more about confidentiality and the fact that their friends attend a particular clinic, while blacks care most about clinic location and the concern of staff for teenagers. Further studies of factors that affect accessibility and how these factors differ by race and age seem warranted. If accessibility is enhanced, this should increase use of clinics by teens. The largest issue with regard to contraception, though, is the demand for services.

Teenagers, black and white, tend to delay obtaining contraception for many months, typically, after they first have sex. Disproportionate numbers of blacks never use birth control, and a large proportion of blacks and whites use birth control inconsistently. Only 35 percent of premaritally sexually active white teens and 31 percent of black teens interviewed in a 1979 national survey indicated that they had consistently used contraception. Among those young women who consistently used a method of contraception, blacks were no more likely to become pregnant than were whites. However, among those who only inconsistently used a method or who never used a method, blacks were more likely to become pregnant.

Exactly why blacks have higher pregnancy rates among inconsistent users and nonusers is not clear and merits further exploration. Young blacks seem to be slightly more fecund than whites, but the difference is very slight past the age of 14. Also, black females report having sex slightly less frequently than whites, so higher frequency presumably is not the explanation. However, blacks initiate sex earlier in general. They are more likely to have sex during the time when they are somewhat more fecund than whites. Also, since early initiators are less likely to use contraception, young black teenagers are more at risk than whites, possibly by a considerable margin, at the youngest ages.

Correct use of a contraceptive method is of course very important to the effectiveness of the method, and given studies reported in Chapter 3 indicating that blacks are somewhat less well-informed than whites, black teens may not be as successful at using contraception. However, the problem of inconsistent use and incorrect or incomplete information is very great among whites as well as blacks.

Reliance on abortion is very high among whites and blacks alike—so high that focusing on further increasing the availability of abortion is not a recommendation to which we can give high priority. Prevention of early pregnancy should be the first goal, we feel. Both delaying the initiation of sexual intercourse and encouraging more consistent use of reliable methods of contraception would help reduce the pregnancy rate. Explanations for the high frequency of unprotected sexual intercourse among teens, particularly black teens, were the focus of the next several chapters.

Education

In chapter 5, "Education as a Motivating Factor," the strong negative association between years of schooling and family size among adults is documented. White, black, and Spanish-origin women who have completed more schooling have fewer children and are more likely to expect to be childless. However, early childbearing has been found to limit educational attainment, and this may account for part of the association. Our goal was to explore whether educational aspirations affect the occurrence of an early birth, and it is clear that they do for both blacks and whites. Teens with high educational aspirations are more likely to postpone initiating sex and to avoid early parenthood. This is the case among black and white teens. Yet it cannot be concluded that low aspirations are the cause of high rates of teenage childbearing among blacks compared to whites. To the contrary, there is a strikingly consistent finding across numerous studies that the educational aspirations of black youth are as high or higher than those of white youth. However, blacks do have lower levels of educational attainment than whites. They also have twice the dropout rate of whites and approximately half of the black women who drop out do so because they are pregnant.

These data suggest that the role for schools and for society in general is not to raise educational aspirations among young blacks but to help them fulfill their already high educational goals. There are many approaches to this goal (and, of course, many reasons to pursue this goal in addition to the prevention of early childbearing). Sex education programs that emphasize the consequences of early childbearing for educational and occupational attainment might help teens appreciate the connection between schooling and pregnancy. Adults may assume that teenagers are aware that an early birth will make continued schooling difficult; teenagers may assume, as they so often seem to do, that they are invulnerable to the misfortunes that befall others. Adults, particularly researchers and policy planners, may also assume that teenagers think rationally about their future, that they see a connection between their current behavior and future well being. Some evidence suggests that students with very high expectations, those who plan to complete college, do make the connection. Others do not. Evidence suggests that the fertility and occupational plans of women become more consistent as women move from their teens into their twenties. Young teens have difficulty seeing a connection between their behavior in the present and their well-being in the future. Can young teens be expected to plan rationally for a faraway occupational future?

Additional complexity is created by the fact that most people have multiple goals. When these goals are in conflict, choices or compromises must be made. Do teens recognize this? Much evidence suggests that teens hide from the implications of their behavior. How consciously or rationally are choices made? Decisions about sexual activity seem to be made on the spur of the moment for many teens. Immediate goals such as social success may be more salient to teenagers than their eventual occupational success, assuming they perceive a conflict in the first place. For all of these reasons, teenagers need to have a better understanding not only of how to prevent a pregnancy, but why it makes sense over the long run for them to avoid early pregnancy. This kind of training should be a part of sex education broadly defined.

A second role for schools and society which would facilitate teens' realization of their educational aspirations and reduce the incidence of adolescent pregnancy would seem to be in keeping teenagers from dropping out. Dropouts are more likely to become pregnant than teens enrolled in school, and therefore reducing dropout rates may reduce the likelihood of pregnancy. Dropouts may be less concerned with preventing pregnancy, though, so encouraging reenrollment and regular attendance may be difficult. Programs that reduce dropout rates, including youth employment and training programs which provide an incentive to stay in school (such as YIEPP, the Youth Incentive Entitlement Pilot Projects), are relevant here. Other programs that help students catch up or stay up with their peers, such as compensatory education, are essential since falling behind in school is strongly correlated with dropping out. Summer programs focusing on academic subjects, job training, and employment should be tried. Special programs could be developed that integrate remedial academic work, sex education, decision-making skills training, and employment readiness training. Traditionally the federal government has played a leading role in these areas. States do not seem to have made these programs a high priority. Therefore, recent cutbacks in federal aid may be counterproductive as far as teenage pregnancy is concerned.

We have noted that low aspirations do not account for the much higher fertility of young blacks, but that low aspirations and dropping out of school are associated with early pregnancy regardless of race. Every school and every school system has students with low aspirations and poor performance. However, some schools contain disproportionate numbers of such students and these schools represent ideal settings for targeted prevention programs focusing on literacy and vocational skills, self esteem and decision-making skills, as well as sex education.

Programs that make education more economically rewarding, that increase the ability of minority group individuals to translate their education into job and career opportunities, may also be important. In a very real sense, the historically limited opportunities available to blacks have undermined the returns to education for blacks. Real opportunities need to be out there or calls for greater education and training will be greeted with cynicism. On the societal level, this implies an improvement in the condition of the economy and continued efforts toward equal economic opportunity. On a more limited level, this would include school-to-work transition programs provided by schools and training centers for recent high school graduates.

School-based programs for teenage mothers should also not be ignored. Young mothers have a very high rate of repeat pregnancy. Programs that keep young mothers in school and provide counseling, sex education, and contraceptive services reduce the incidence of early second pregnancies. Such programs are essential because, while achievement is handicapped by having one child, the burdens associated with caring for two young children are frequently overwhelming.

Employment and Job Training

Chapter 6, "Employment and Job Training," reviews the few studies that have been done exploring whether teenagers' occupational aspirations and job opportunities affect their fertility behavior. The studies that have been done have produced conflicting results. However, data for the late 1970s indicate that the occupational aspirations of black youth are as high as those of white youth, undercutting the argument that low aspirations explain the high incidence of early sexual activity and pregnancy among black youth. Nevertheless, ancedotal evidence does suggest that youth who feel they have no future are particularly apt to feel apathetic about family planning (Haffner, 1983). Our own interviews with high school students suggest that among black males occupational aspirations do not affect sexual behavior but may increase the use of contraception. The paucity of research on this topic is so great that we hope to see more work on this issue, for males as well as for females.

Studies of youth who have participated in job training programs do provide evidence, on the other hand, that participants have lower fertility than comparable youth who do not receive job training. Perhaps the training experience makes more clear to participants what is involved in obtaining and keeping a good job.

In general, the aspirations of youth seem very high with half planning to finish college and nearly half aspiring to a high-status white-collar occupation among both blacks and whites. A lack of information and experience may account for the fact that so many teens engage in behaviors that jeopardize their life aspirations.

Marriage and Family

Chapter 7, "Marriage and Family," explores the marriage patterns of blacks compared to whites and Spanish-origin Americans and considers the causes and implications of the very different patterns.

The marriages of black adults tend to end in separation, divorce, or widowhood with far greater regularity than do the marriages of whites or Spanish-origin couples. Although most blacks define marriage as very important to them and the vast majority of black youth plan to marry, blacks do not rank marriage as highly as whites do. In addition, black women rate economic factors as more important than companionship as a reason for marriage; blacks prefer to be older when they marry; blacks are more likely to dissolve their marriages even when social and economic factors are held constant; and a significant proportion of black youth indicates that their desired age for having a first child is earlier than their desired age at marriage. Thus important racial differences exist in patterns of marriage and in attitudes about marriage. These differences appear to arise from the disadvantaged social and economic position of blacks.

Economic factors, including high unemployment and low income, appear to undermine the ability of blacks to form and maintain stable marriages. Welfare, though it does not appear to be an incentive to early parenthood or marital disruption, represents a source of stable income and health coverage in Medicaid, and thus welfare may compare favorably with marriage in that segment of the population unable to obtain steady employment with fringe benefits and reasonable wages. Black families are both larger and poorer than white families, and this may make it more difficult for them to subsidize early marriage. However, black families do tend to provide considerable assistance to young mothers, though whether this poses an incentive to early, out-of-wedlock motherhood or represents an adjustment to early motherhood is not known.

One factor that may have had a profound effect on black marriage patterns and male-female relationships is the imbalance in the black sex ratio. Due to higher mortality, more frequent institutionalization, and higher rates of unemployment, black women face a shortage of marriageable black men. Thus black women seeking to establish or maintain a stable marriage are in a more vulnerable position than are white women.

Black youth seem to have reacted to this reality of black marriage patterns with attitudes that are less positive toward marriage, more accepting of premarital sex, more tolerant of out-of-wedlock parenthood, and, for some, attitudes that favor earlier childbearing than marriage. Although studies that disentangle the causal association do not exist, it seems unlikely that causality runs from negative attitudes regarding marriage to lower wages, higher unemployment, and an imbalanced sex ratio. Consequently we assume that any relationship that exists goes from the social and economic realities of adult marriage patterns to the attitudes youth hold toward marriage and family formation.

In 1982, only 42 percent of black children under age 18 were living in families with two parents, compared to 81 percent of white children and 69 percent of Spanish-origin children. Teens in one-parent homes are more likely to be sexually experienced and to become parents at a young age; but the explanation for this association is not clear. Black single-parent families are particularly likely to be poor and therefore black children are particularly likely to grow up in low-income homes in low-income neighborhoods. Residing in an economically depressed neighborhood has been linked to earlier sexual activity and pregnancy. Children in one-parent homes may also be exposed to parental dating and may be less well-supervised than children with two parents to share the task. Although research has not established a causal link between number of parents in the home and these variables, close supervision has been found to predict a lower probability of early sexual activity and pregnancy. Other research has found that girls from two-parent families are less likely to feel that premarital intercourse is always all right and are less likely to have had premarital intercourse. Thus, family structure does seem to have implications for the greater exposure of black teens to early pregnancy.

Since the social and economic liabilities that have constrained blacks are unlikely to disappear immediately, a realistic approach to the problem of early pregnancy in the black community will need to confront the attitudes of contemporary black youth which seem to be relatively accepting of early sex and out-of-wedlock parenthood. However, it is important to recognize that blacks, like other social groups, are very heterogeneous and that the adult generation does not support or encourage early sexual activity or pregnancy. Messages that encourage early sex are received by teens from their peers and the media, as well as from their maturing bodies. Teens need to receive information and opinions that counter the misinformation and incomplete information they have about sex and pregnancy and the pressure to have sex at a young age that they receive from so many sides.

Additional Research

Many shortcomings in our understanding undermine our ability to reach more definitive conclusions. One particular gap is the almost complete neglect of the role of the male teenager in the existing research literature. How the sexual and contraceptive behaviors of males are affected by their attitudes, aspirations, experiences, and values has only begun to be researched. The male partner clearly wields substantial influence, yet how and why are not understood; nor is it clear how best to reach young males. Another important gap in the research literature pertains to Hispanic teenagers. Studies of Hispanics are almost nonexistent. Despite some agreement that Hispanics place great importance on families, almost no research has been done on sex, fertility, and marriage among Hispanic teens. In addition, studies that do not simply look at black-white differences but explore differences within the black community are uncommon. Studies of families who manage to protect their adolescents from precocious sexual activity and pregnancy despite social and economic obstacles should be initiated. Studies that carefully control for racial differences in social and economic status are also in short supply. Future researchers should use multiple indicators of social and economic status.

In general, more research is needed on sex education—how to introduce sex education into a community, what to cover at particular ages, how to clarify the effect that sex and pregnancy can have on one's life plans, how to involve males in pregnancy prevention, how to help teens determine whether they are ready to have sex and to resist peer pressure until they are. Research on the effects of the media and ways to innoculate youth to media influences is also needed.

Exploration of how the issue of adolescent pregnancy is like other adolescent problems—drinking, drugs, running away, etc.—and what common solutions exist should also be fruitful. Researchers and service providers working on similar adolescent problems could share their understanding and reduce the need for each group to "reinvent the wheel." In addition, consideration of approaches taken in other countries might suggest policies and programs that would be effective in the United States as well.

Conclusions

In terms of our original hypotheses regarding information, services, and motivation, we have reached several conclusions. One is that the role of information is very important, particularly if information is defined broadly to include information about the consequences of a birth for one's future life. The absence of information poses a barrier to teens' ability to understand the implications of their behavior and to implement the conclusions they reach. More information about conception and contraception is needed, particularly by boys, blacks, and youth from low socioeconomic families, but more generally by all youth. However, sex education needs to encompass more than just information about sex. Decision-making skills, means-ends thinking, resistance to peer pressures and media influences, and communication skills need to be taught, as well as the relevance of pregnancy to the achievement of educational and occupational aspirations.

In terms of services, it appears that blacks and whites alike need more available and accessible services, since only about half of black and white teens in need of services are served. Recent budget cuts may have increased the need for services somewhat. Again, the absence or inaccessibility of services poses a barrier to those sexually active teens who want to prevent pregnancy. The greater need, however, is to increase teenagers' perception that they need services and their willingness to obtain services and use them consistently. Because so many blacks initiate sex early in their teen years, they may be particularly hard to reach in terms of information and services. Older teens are more effective contraceptors and efforts to encourage young teens to delay having sex seem warranted for the very practical reason that young teens are particularly ineffective contraceptors.

Whatever one's personal attitudes concerning the appropriateness of sexual activity for teenagers of different ages, it should be clear that there are many pragmatic reasons to discourage early initiation of sexual activity. Parents, schools, and community institutions alike will need to work to bring home the reality of early and out-of-wedlock childbearing in an attempt to counterbalance the "it can't happen to me" nonchalance of so many youth. Instead of withholding information in the belief that information causes promiscuity, adults need to provide more information and a broader array of information to youth and children. It would also appear that adults need to take a position against too-early sexual activity. Although a consensus regarding the appropriate age for initiating sexual activity seems unlikely, one thing does seem clear. At present, black youth don't just start early; they start too early in terms of responsible contraceptive behavior. The trend for white youth is in the same direction, suggesting that while the black community may need to take leadership, whites should also consider how to encourage young teens to delay having intercourse.

Considering the role of aspirations, it does not appear that blacks have lower educational or occupational aspirations than whites. High aspirations do seem to lead youth to delay sex or avoid pregnancy; but this is true among both blacks and whites, and differences in aspirations do not seem to explain the higher fertility of young blacks.

While black and white youth seem to have comparable aspirations for schooling and occupational attainment, attitudes about family formation do differ by race. Black youth seem to have more liberal attitudes about premarital sex and out-of-wedlock pregnancy and prefer to be younger when they have their first child. Black youth are also more likely to be raised in single-parent families. Since this family type has been linked with more frequent early sexual activity and more permissive attitudes toward premarital sexual activity, the high incidence of one-parent homes in the black community may be a factor in the higher incidence of teenage pregnancy in the black community.

It should also be noted explicitly that social and economic disadvantages tend to go hand in hand. Low levels of educational attainment, unemployment, poverty, and single parenthood are *not* isolated phenomena. Black youth are more often exposed to several disposing factors, and the joint occurrence of these factors seems likely to substantially elevate the risk of early pregnancy. Though we have explored them separately, implicitly implying that their effects are additive, it may be that their effects are multiplicative. That is, the joint effect of living in a neighborhood with a high dropout rate and high unemployment and being a member of a low-income, single-parent household may be considerably stronger than the effect of the three factors occurring separately.

After reviewing the available research, we have identified a set of issues for action or further research on the basis of a model that explores information, services, and aspirations as if they were separate issues, whereas they are inevitably intertwined. In addition, we have explored educational, employment, and family patterns as if they were discrete areas of life, and of course they are not. It is crucial to emphasize that the pieces that we have tried to dissect for analytic purposes really do make a whole, and that that whole is represented by the differential social position, both currently and historically, of blacks in American life. Black-white differences in teenage fertility would probably not exist, in our view, if blacks currently and historically had enjoyed social and economic equality with whites; but they have not. Since the higher incidence of teenage childbearing in the black community seems to mitigate achieving such equality, it seems essential to address this issue as one part of broader efforts to achieve a more equal society. Similarly, as blacks experience greater economic and social equality, the prominence of early parenthood among blacks should diminish.

References

Abrams, Doris L. 1980. "Women's Educational Attainment and Fertility." Paper presented at the Annual Convention of the American Psychological Association, September 1–5.

Alan Guttmacher Institute. 1983. "School Sex Education in Policy and Practice." *Public Policy Issues in Brief* 3(3).

———. 1982. *Current Functioning and Future Priorities in Family Planning Services Delivery*. New York: The Alan Guttmacher Institute.

———. 1981. *Teenage Pregnancy: The Problem That Hasn't Gone Away*. New York: The Alan Guttmacher Institute.

Almquist, E. Mc. 1979. *Minorities, Gender and Work*. Lexington, Mass.: D.C. Heath.

Anderson, John. 1977. "Planning of Births: Difference between Blacks and Whites in the United States," *Phylon*, 38(3) 282–96.

Anderson, Kristine. 1980. "Educational Goals of Male and Female Adolescents: The Effects of Parental Characteristics and Attitudes." *Youth and Society* 12: 173–88.

Arce, Carole. 1982. "Maintaining a Group Culture." *IRS Newsletter*, (Winter).

Baldwin, Wendy. 1980. "The Fertility of Young Adolescents." *Journal of Adolescent Health Care* 1(1): 54–59.

Ballard, Charles. 1983. Personal communication.

Bane, Mary Jo, and David T. Ellwood. 1983. "The Dynamics of Dependence: The Routes to Self-Sufficiency," Cambridge, Mass.: Urban Systems Research and Engineering.

———. 1983. "Slipping into and out of Poverty: The Dynamics of Spells," Harvard University. Unpublished paper.

Bauman, Karl, and J. Richard Udry. 1981. "Subjective Expected Utility and Adolescent Sexual Behavior." *Adolescence* 16: 527–35.

Bernardik, E., P.B. Namerow, and M. Weinstein. 1982. "Does a Prior Pregnancy Affect Choice of Contraceptive Method or Effectiveness of Use?" Paper presented at the annual meeting of the American Public Health Association, Montreal, and reported in "Digest," *Family Planning Perspectives* 15(3): 137–38.

Biddle, Bruce, Barbara Bank, and Marjorie Marlin. 1980. "Parental and Peer Influence on Adolescents." *Social Forces* 58(4): 1057–79.

Billy, John, and Richard Udry. 1983. "The Effects of Age and Pubertal Development on Adolescent Sexual Behavior." Chapel Hill: University of North Carolina, Carolina Population Center.

Billy, John, Joseph Rodgers, and J. Richard Udry. 1981. "Adolescent Sexual Behavior and Friendship Choice." Chapel Hill: University of North Carolina, Carolina Population Center.

141

Blake, Judith. 1982. "Sociological Perspectives on Population Studies." In Robert Schoen and David Landman eds., *Population: Theory and Policy*. Urbana-Champaign: University of Illinois.

———. 1970. "Demographic Science and the Redirection of Public Policy." In T. Ford and G. De Jong, (eds.), *Social Demography*, Englewood Cliffs, NJ: Prentice-Hall: 326–47.

Blake, Judith, and Joyce Del Pinal. 1982. "Educational Attainment and Reproductive Preferences: Theory and Evidence." In *Determinants of Fertility Trends: Theories Reexamined*. Charlotte Hohn and Ranier Mackensen eds. Liege: Ordina Editions.

Block, Harvey. 1981. "Welfare Costs at the Local Level." Final Report to National Institute of Child Health and Human Development.

Bloom, David, and James Trussell. 1983. "What Are the Determinants of Delayed Childbearing and Permanent Childlessness in the United States?" National Bureau of Economic Research, Inc., Working Paper 1140.

Borders, Jeff, and Phillips Cutright. 1979. "Community Determinants of U.S. Legal Abortion Rates." *Family Planning Perspectives* 11(4): 227–33.

Borker, Susan, Julia Loughlin, and Claire Rudolph. 1979. "The Long-Term Effects of Adolescent Childrearing: A Retrospective Analysis." *Journal of Social Service Research* 2(4): 341–55.

Borus, Michael E., ed. 1983. *Tomorrow's Workers*. Lexington, Mass.: D.C. Heath.

Borus, Michael E., Joan E. Crowley, Russell W. Rumberger, Richard Santos, and David Shapiro. 1980. *Pathways to the Future: A Longitudinal Study of Young Americans; Preliminary Report: Youth and the Labor Market—1979*. Columbus, Ohio: Center for Human Resource Research, The Ohio State University.

Bould, Sally. 1977. "Black and White Families: Factors Affecting the Wife's Contribution to the Family Income Where the Husband's Income Is Low to Moderate." *The Sociological Quarterly* 18(Autumn): 536–47.

Bronfenbrenner, Urie. 1979. *The Ecology of Human Development*. Cambridge, Mass.: Harvard University Press.

Brown, Prudence. 1983. "The Swedish Approach to Sex Education and Adolescent Pregnancy: Some Impressions." *Family Planning Perspectives* 15(2): 90–95.

Bumpass, Larry, and Ronald Rindfuss. 1982. "The Effect of Marital Dissolution on Contraception Protection." Working Paper 82-56. Center for Demography and Ecology, Madison: The University of Wisconsin.

Bumpass, Larry, Ronald Rindfuss, and Richard Janosik. 1978. "Age and Marital Status at First Birth and the Pace of Subsequent Fertility." *Demography* 15: 75–86.

Byrne, E. and William Fisher. *Adolescents, Sex and Contraception*. Hillsdale, N.J.: Lawrence Erlbaum Assoc.: 273-300.

Card, Josefina J. 1977. *Long-Term Consequences for Children Born to Adolescent Parents*. Final report to the National Institute of Child Health and Human Development. Palo Alto, California: American Institutes for Research.

Card, Josefina J., and Lauress L. Wise. 1978. "Teenage Mothers and Teenage Fathers: The Impact of Early Childbearing on the Parents' Personal and Professional Lives." *Family Planning Perspectives* 10(July/August): 199–205.

Carley, Susan. 1978. "Discrimination: Separating Race Effects from the Effects of Social Class." Paper presented at 1978 Meetings of the Southern Sociological Society, New Orleans.

Carlson, Elwood. 1979. "Family Background, School and Early Marriage." *Journal of Marriage and the Family.* 41(2): 341–53.

Carlson, Elwood, and Kandi Stinson. 1982. "Motherhood, Marriage Timing, and Marital Stability: A Research Note." *Social Forces* 61(1): 258–67.

Carson, Emmett D. 1983. "Possible Approaches for Social Science Research on the Underclass." Paper presented to the Population Association of America.

Cazenave, Noel A. 1983. "Black Male-Black Female Relationships: The Perceptions of 155 Middle-Class Black Men." *Family Relations* 32(July): 341–50.

Center for Human Resource Research. 1982. *Pathways to the Future*, Vol. 2, A Final Report on the National Longitudinal Survey of Youth Labor Market Experience in 1980. Columbus, Ohio: College of Administrative Science, Ohio State University.

Chamie, Mary, and Stanley Henshaw. 1981. "The Costs and Benefits of Government Expenditures for Family Planning Programs," *Family Planning Perspectives* 13(3): 117–24.

Chapman, Bruce. 1982. "The Northwest Version of a Changing America." Remarks to the Seattle Rotary Club.

Cherlin, Andrew. 1981. *Marriage, Divorce, Remarriage: Social Trends in the United States.* Cambridge, Mass.: Harvard University Press.

———. 1980. "Postponing Marriage: The Influence of Young Women's Work Expectations." *Journal of Marriage and the Family* 42(2): 355–65.

Chilman, Catherine S. 1983. *Adolescent Sexuality in a Changing American Society.* New York: Wiley.

———. 1979. *Adolescent Sexuality in a Changing American Society—Social and Psychological Perspectives.* Washington, D.C.: U.S. Department of Health, Education and Welfare, Public Health Service, National Institutes of Health.

Clark, Samuel, Laurie Zabin, and Janet Hardy. 1984. "Sex Contraception and Parenthood: Experience and Attitudes Among Urban Black Young Men." *Family Planning Perspectives* 16(2): 77–82.

Cobliner, W.G. 1981. "Prevention of Adolescent Pregnancy: A Developmental Perspective." In E. McAnarney and G. Stickle, Eds., *Pregnancy and Childbearing during Adolescence: Research Priorities for the 1980s.* New York: Alan Liss.: 35–47.

Combs, Michael W., and Susan Welch. 1982. "Blacks, Whites, and Attitudes toward Abortion." *Public Opinion Quarterly* 46: 510–20.

Conley, Martha M. 1976. "Family Life and Sex Education Among Low-Income Families." Paper presented at the Conference on the Urban South. Norfolk, Virginia.

Cramer, James. 1980. "Fertility and Female Employment: Problems of Causal Direction." *American Sociological Review* 45(2): 397–432.

Crosbie, Paul and Dianne Bitte. 1982. "A Test of Luker's Theory of Contraceptive Risk-Taking." *Studies in Family Planning* 13(3): 67–78.

Crowley, Joan E., and David Shapiro. 1982. "Aspirations and Expectations of Youth in the United States. Part 1: Education and Fertility." *Youth and Society* 13(June): 391–422.

Cummings, Michele, and Scott Cummings. 1983. "Family Planning Among the Urban Poor: Sexual Politics and Social Policy." *Family Relations* 32(January): 47–58.

Curtis, Russell L., Jr. 1975. "Adolescent Orientations Toward Parents and Peers: Variations by Sex, Age, and Socioeconomic Status." *Adolescence* 10(Winter): 483–94.

Cutright, Phillips, and Frederick S. Jaffe. 1976. "Family Planning Program Effects on the Fertility of Low-Income U.S. Women." *Family Planning Perspectives* 8(May/June): 100–110.

Cvetkovich, George and Barbara Grote. 1980. "Male Teenagers—Sexual Debut, Psychosocial Development and Contraceptive Use." Paper presented at the 88th Annual Convention of the American Psychological Association, Montreal.

Cvetkovich, George, Barbara Grote, Ann Bjorseth and Julia Sarkissian. 1975. "On the Psychology of Adolescents' Use of Contraceptives." *The Journal of Sex Research* 11:256–70.

Danziger, Sheldon, George Jakubson, Saul Schwartz, and Eugene Smolensky. 1982. "Work and Welfare as Determinants of Female Poverty and Household Headship." *Quarterly Journal of Economics* 97(3): 519–34.

Darabi, Katherine. 1982. "Sex-Related Knowledge, Attitudes and Behavior of Hispanic Teenagers in New York City." Paper presented at meetings of the American Public Health Association, Montreal, Canada.

Davies, Mark and Denise B. Kandel. 1981. "Parental and Peer Influences on Adolescents' Educational Plans: Some Further Evidence." *American Journal of Sociology* 87(2): 363–87.

Delcampo, Robert, Michael Sporakowski, and Diana Delcampo. 1976. "Premarital Sexual Permissiveness and Contraceptive Knowledge: A Biracial Comparison of College Students." *The Journal of Sex Research* 12(3): 180–92.

Devaney, Barbara, and Katherine Hubley. 1981. "The Determinants of Adolescent Pregnancy and Childbearing." Final Report to the Center for Population Research, National Institute of Child Health and Human Development. Washington, D.C.: Mathematica Policy Research.

Dryfoos, Joy, and Toni Heiser. 1978. "Contraceptive Services for Adolescents: An Overview." *Family Planning Perspectives* 10(4): 223–233.

Elkind, D. 1967. "Egocentrism in Adolescence." *Child Development* 38: 1025–34.

Espenshade, Thomas J. 1982. "Marriage, Divorce, and Remarriage from Retrospective Data: A Multiregional Approach." Paper presented at the meetings of the Population Association of America.

Ezzard, N.V., W. Cates, Jr., D.G. Kramer, and C. Tietze. 1982. "Race-Specific Patterns of Abortion Use by American Teenagers." *American Journal of Public Health* 72: 809.

Farley, J. 1970. "Graduate Women: Career Aspirations and Desired Family Size." *American Psychologist* 25: 1099–1100.

Farrell, Walter, Marvin Dawkins, and Shirley Eves. 1978. "Sexual Attitudes and Knowledge among Black Inner-City Elementary School Students in Philadelphia: A Pilot Study." Paper presented at the National Sex Institute of the American Association of Sex Education, Counselors and Therapists, Washington, D.C.

Field, Barry. 1981. "A Socio-Economic Analysis of Out-of-Wedlock Births among Teenagers." In K. Scott, T. Field, and E. Robertson eds., *Teenage Parents and Their Offspring*. New York: Grume and Stratton: 15–33.

Finkel, Madelon Lubin, and David J. Finkel. 1975. "Sexual and Contraceptive Knowledge, Attitudes and Behavior of Male Adolescents." *Family Planning Perspectives* 7(November/December): 156–260.

Forrest, Jacqueline D. 1980. *Exploration of the Effects of Organized Family Planning Programs in the United States on Adolescent Fertility*. Final Report to the Center for Population Research, National Institutes of Health.

Forrest, Jacqueline D., Albert Hermalin, and Stanley Henshaw. 1981. "The Impact of Family Planning Clinic Programs on Adolescent Pregnancy." *Family Planning Perspectives* 13(3): 109–16.

Fox, Greer, Bruce Fox, and Katherine Frohardt-Lane. 1982. "Fertility Socialization." In G. Fox ed. *The Childbearing Decision*. Beverly Hills: Sage: 19–49.

Fox, Greer Litton. 1980. "The Mother-Adolescent Daughter Relationship as a Sexual Socialization Structure: A Research Review." *Family Relations* 29 (January): 21–28.

Fox, Greer Litton and Judith Inazu. 1980. "Patterns and Outcomes of Mother-Daughter Communication about Sexuality." *Journal of Social Issues* 36(1): 7–29.

Fox, Greer. 1975. "Sex Role Attitudes as Predictors of Contraceptive Use." Paper presented at meetings of the National Council on Family Relations, Salt Lake City.

Freedman, Ronald, P.K. Whelpton, and A.A. Campbell. 1959. *Family Planning, Sterility, and Population Control*. New York: McGraw-Hill.

Freeman, Ellen, Karl Rickels, Emily Mudd, and George Huggins. 1982. "Never-Pregnant Adolescents and Family Planning Programs: Contraception, Continuation, and Pregnancy Risk." *American Journal of Public Health* 72(8): 815–22.

Freeman, Ellen, Karl Rickels, Emily Mudd, George Huggins, and Celso-Ramon Garcia. 1982b. "Self-Reports of Emotional Distress in a Sample of Urban Black High School Students." *Psychological Medicine* 12: 809–17.

Freeman, Ellen, Karl Rickels, George Huggins, Emily Mudd, Celso-Ramon Garcia, and Helen Dickens. 1980. "Adolescent Contraceptive Use: Comparison of Male and Female Attitudes and Information." *American Journal of Public Health* 70(August): 790–97.

Frese, Wolfgang. 1982. "The Effects of Two Generations of Status Attainments on Educational Aspirations for Offspring." Paper presented at Southern Association of Agricultural Scientists, Orlando, Florida.

Fuchs, Victor. 1983. *How We Live*. Cambridge: Harvard University Press.

Furstenberg, Frank, Judy Shea, Paul Allison, Robert Herceg-Baron, and David Webb. 1983. "Patterns of Contraceptive Use among Adolescent Clients in Family Planning Clinics: A Longitudinal Study." Paper presented at the annual meetings of the Population Association of America, Pittsburgh, April.

Furstenberg, Frank. 1971. "Birth Control Experience among Pregnant Adolescents: The Process of Unplanned Parenthood." *Social Problems* 19: 192–203.

George, Valerie. 1981. "Occupational Aspirations of Talented Black and White Adolescent Females." *Journal of Nonwhite Concerns*, July: 137–45.

Gibbs, James O., Phyllis A. Ewer, and Rebecca B. Bahr. 1976. "Racial Differences in Attitudes toward Marriage and Unwed Childbearing." *International Journal of Sociology of the Family* 5(2): 243–48.

Gilchrist, Lewayne, and Steven Schinke. 1983. "Teenage Pregnancy and Public Policy." *Social Service Review* (June): 307–22.

Gispert, Maria, and Ruth Falk. 1976. "Sexual Experimentation and Pregnancy in Young Black Adolescents." *American Journal of Obstetrics and Gynecology* (October): 459–66.

Granberg, Donald and Beth Wellman Granberg. 1981. "Pro-Life Versus Pro-Choice: Another Look at the Abortion Controversy in the U.S." *Sociology and Social Research* 65(4): 424–34.

Groeneveld, Lyle P. 1980. *The Effects of the SIME/DIME Manpower Treatments on Marital Stability, Fertility, and Migration*. Menlo Park, CA: SRI International.

Gunderson, Mark, and James McCary. 1980. "Effects of Sex Education on Sex Information and Sexual Guilt, Attitudes and Behaviors." *Family Relations* 29(3): 357–79.

Guttentag, Marcia, and Paul Secord. 1983. *Too Many Women? The Sex Ratio Question*. Beverly Hills: Sage.

Haffner, Debbie. 1983. Personal communication.

Haggstrom, Gus W., D.E. Kanouse, and Peter .A. Morrison. 1981. *Teenage Parents: Their Ambitions and Attainments*. Santa Monica, Calif.: The Rand Corporation (R-2771-NICHD).

Haggstrom, Gus W. and Peter A. Morrison. 1979. "Consequences of Parenthood in Late Adolescence: Findings from the National Longitudinal Study of High School Seniors." Santa Monica, Calif.: The Rand Corporation.

Hamilton, Stephen and Ann Crouter. 1980. "Work and Growth: A Review of Research on the Impact of Work Experience on Adolescent Development." *Journal of Youth and Adolescence* 9(4): 323–38.

Harlan, William, Elizabeth Harlan, and George Grillo. 1980. "Secondary Sex Characteristics of Girls 12 to 17 Years of Age: The U.S. Health Examination Survey." *The Journal of Pediatrics* 96(6): 1074–78.

Harlan, William, George Grillo, Joan Carnoni-Huntley, and Paul Leaverton. 1979. "Secondary Sex Characteristics of Boys 12 to 17 Years of Age: The U.S. Health Examination Survey." *The Journal of Pediatrics* 95(2): 293–97.

Harris, William, Castellano Turner, and William Darity. 1981. "Black Family Planning: Attitudes of Leaders and a General Sample." Paper presented at the 39th Annual Meeting of the American Psychological Association, Los Angeles, California.

Harrison, Algea. 1981. "Attitudes toward Procreation among Black Adults." In H. McAdoo, ed., *Black Families*. Beverly Hills: Sage, 199–208.

Hartley, Shirley Foster. 1975. *Illegitimacy*. Berkeley, Calif.: The University of California Press.

Hatcher, Sherry Lynn Marcus. 1973. "The Adolescent Experience of Pregnancy and Abortion: A Developmental Analysis." *Journal of Youth and Adolescence* 2(1): 52–102.

Hatchet, Shirley. 1983. Personal communication.

Heiss, Jerold. 1981. "Women's Values Regarding Marriage and the Family." In H. McAdoo, ed., *Black Families*. Beverly Hills: Sage, 186–97.

Hendricks, Leo E. 1980. "Black Unwed Adolescent Fathers." *Urban Research Review* 6(1): 7–9.

Henshaw, Stanley, and Kevin O'Reilly. 1983. "Characteristics of Abortion Patients in the United States, 1979 and 1980." *Family Planning Perspectives* 15 (January/February): 5–16.

Henshaw, Stanley, and Greg Martire. 1982. "Abortion and the Public Opinion Polls 1. Mortality and Legality." *Family Planning Perspectives* 14(2) (March/April): 53–60.

Henshaw, Stanley, Jacqueline D. Forrest, Ellen Sullivan, and Christopher Tietz. 1981. "Abortion in the United States, 1978-1979." *Family Planning Perspectives* 13(January/February): 6–18.

Herold, E. 1980. "Contraceptive Attitudes and Behavior of Single Adolescent Females." Final Report to National Institute of Child Health and Human Development.

Herold, Edward, Marilyn Godwin, and Donna Lero. 1979. "Self-esteem, Locus of Control and Adolescent Contraception." *Journal of Psychology* 101:83–88.

Hill, Martha, and Michael Ponza. 1983. "Poverty Across Generations: Is Welfare Dependency a Pathology Passed from One Generation to the Next?" Unpublished manuscript.

Hirsch, Marilyn, and Melvin Zelnik. 1982. "Contraceptive Method Switching Among American Female Adolescents." Paper presented at the American Public Health Meetings, Montreal, Canada.

Hobbs, Daniel F., Jr., and Jane Maynard Wimbish. 1977. "Transition to Parenthood of Black Couples." *Journal of Marriage and the Family* 39 (November): 677–89.

Hofferth, Sandra L. 1983. "Updating Children's Life Course." Washington, D.C.: The Urban Institute.

------. 1981. "Effects of Number and Timing of Births on Family Well-Being Over the Life Cycle." Final Report to the National Institute of Child Health and Human Development under Contract Number NO1-HD-82850. Washington, D.C.: The Urban Institute.

Hofferth, Sandra L., and Kristin A. Moore. 1979. "Early Childbearing and Later Economic Well-Being." *American Sociological Review* 44(October): 784–815.

Hoffman, Lois, Arland Thornton, and Jean Manis. 1978. "The Value of Children to Parents in the United States." *Journal of Population* 1 (Summer): 91–131.

Hogan, Dennis, and Evelyn Kitagawa. 1983. "Family Factors in the Fertility of Black Adolescents." Paper presented at annual meetings of the Population Association of America.

Hong, Lawrence K. 1974. "The Instability of Teenage Marriage in the United States: An Evaluation of the Socio-economic Status Hypothesis." *International Journal of Sociology of the Family* 4(2): 201–12.

Horowitz, Rick. 1981. "Should Contraceptives Be Advertised on Television?" *Channels of Communication* 1(October/November): 64–66.

Hout, Michael. 1978. "The Determinants of Marital Fertility in the United States, 1968-70: Inferences from a Dynamic Model. *"Demography* 15(2): 139–60.

Howard University Institute for Urban Affairs and Research. 1980. "The Black Male: A Statistical Profile." *Urban Research Review* 6(1): 1–4.

Howell, Frank M., and Wolfgang Frese. 1982. "Adult Role Transitions, Parental Influence, and Status Aspirations Early in the Life Course." *Journal of Marriage and the Family* (February): 35–48.

------. 1982. "Early Transition into Adult Roles: Some Antecedents and Outcomes." *American Educational Research Journal* 19(Spring): 51–73.

------. 1981. "Educational Plans as Motivation or Attitude? Some Additional Evidence." *Social Psychology Quarterly* 44(3): 218–36.

------. 1979. "Race, Sex, and Aspirations: Evidence for the 'Race Convergence' Hypothesis." *Sociology of Education* 52(January): 34–46.

------. 1978. "Parental Influence on Achievement Attitudes: Longitudinal Race-Sex Estimates." Paper presented at the Annual Meeting of the Rural Sociological Society.

Hudis, Paula, and Jan Brazzell. 1981. "Significant Others, Adult Role Expectations, and the Resolution of Teenage Pregnancies." In Paul Ahmed, ed. *Pregnancy, Childbirth and Parenthood.* New York: Elsevier: 167–87.

Jackson, Jacquelyne. 1978. "But Where Are the Men?" In R. Staples ed. *The Black Family.* Belmont, Calif.: Wadsworth.

Jackson, Roberta. 1981. "Some Aspirations of Lower Class Black Mothers." In George Kurian ed. *Women in the Family and the Economy: An International Comparative Survey.* Westport, Conn.: Greenwood Press.

Jenkins, Rene. 1983. Final Report to the National Institute of Child Health and Human Development. Washington, D.C.: Howard University Hospital.

Jessor, Richard, Frances Costa, Lee Jessor, and John E. Donovan. 1983. "Timing of First Intercourse: A Prospective Study." *Journal of Personality and Social Psychology* 44(3): 608–26.

Jessor, Shirley, and Richard Jessor. 1975. "Transition from Virginity to Nonvirginity among Youth." *Developmental Psychology* 11(4): 473–84.

Johnson, Leanor. 1983. Personal Communication.

Johnson, Shirley and Londell Snow. 1982. "Assessment of Reproductive Knowledge in an Inner-City Clinic." *Social Science Medicine* 16: 1657–62.

Jones, Judith, P.B. Namerow, and S.G. Philliber. 1982. "Adolescents' Use of a Hospital-Based Contraceptive Program" *Family Planning Perspectives* 14(4): 224–30.

Jorgensen, Stephen R. 1981. "Sex Education and the Reduction of Adolescent Pregnancies: Prospects for the 1980s." *Journal of Early Adolescence* 1(1): 38–52.

Juhasz, Anne, and Mary Sonnenshein-Schneider. 1980. "Adolescent Sexual Decision-Making: Components and Skills." *Adolescence* 15(60): 743–50.

Kantner, John, and Melvin Zelnik. 1973. "Contraception and Pregnancy: Experience of Young Unmarried Women in the United States," *Family Planning Perspectives* 5(1): 11–25.

Kantner, John, and Melvin Zelnik. 1972. "Sexual Experience of Young Unmarried Women in the United States." *Family Planning Perspectives* 4(4): 9–18

Kenkel, W.F. 1985. "Change and Stability in the Occupational Plans of Females." In Sarah Shaffner and William F. Kenkel, eds., *On the Road to Adulthood*. Greensboro, N.C.: University of North Carolina, North Carolina Agricultural Research Service.

Kenkel, William. 1982. "Middle Childhood Antecedents of Age at Marriage Expectations Among Low-Income Females." *Sociological Focus* 15(1): 53–65.

Kenkel, William F. 1981. "Black-White Differences in Age at Marriage: Expectations of Low Income High School Girls." *The Journal of Negro Education* 50(4): 425–38.

Kerckhoff, Alan, and Alan Parrow. 1979. "The Effect of Early Marriage on the Educational Attainment of Young Men." *Journal of Marriage and the Family* 41(1): 97–107.

Kimmich, Madeleine H., Jane Goldmuntz, Freya L. Sonenstein, and Martha R. Burt. 1983. "Helping Pregnant Adolescents: Outcomes and Costs of Service Delivery, Draft Final Report on the Evaluation of Adolescent Pregnancy Programs." Washington, D.C.: The Urban Institute.

Kirby, Douglas S. 1984. *Sexuality Education: An Evaluation of Programs and Their Effects*. Santa Cruz, California: Network Publications.

Kirby, Douglas, and Judith Alter. 1980. "The Experts Rate Important Features and Outcomes of Sex Education Programs." *Journal of School Health* (November): 497–502.

Kirby, Douglas, J. Alter, and P. Scales. 1979. "An Analysis of U.S. Sex Education Programs and Evaluation Methods." Washington, D.C.: U.S. Department of Health, Education and Welfare.

Koenig, Michael, and Melvin Zelnik. 1982. "The Risk of Premarital First Pregnancy among Metropolitan-Area Teenagers." *Family Planning Perspectives* 14(5): 239–47.

Koo, Helen, and Richard Bilsborrow. 1979. "Multivariate Analyses of Effects of Age at First Birth: Results from the 1973 National Survey of Family Growth and 1975 Current Population Survey." Paper prepared for the National Institute of Child Health and Human Development under Contract Number HD-62859.

Kuvlesky, William P., and Angelita S. Obordo. 1972. "A Racial Comparison of Teenage Girls' Projections for Marriage and Procreation." *Journal of Marriage and the Family* 34 (February): 75–84.

Ladner, Joyce A. 1971. *Tomorrow's Tomorrow: The Black Woman.* Garden City: Doubleday and Company, Inc.

Leibowitz, Arleen, Marvin Eisen, and Winston Chow. 1980. "Decision Making in Teenage Pregnancy: An Analysis of Choice." Paper presented at the annual meetings of the Population Association of America, Denver.

Levy, S. B., with W. J. Grinker. 1983. *Choices and Life Circumstances: An Ethnographic Study of Project Redirection Teens.* New York, New York: Manpower Demonstration Research Corporation.

Lindemann, Constance. 1974. *Birth Control and Unmarried Young Women.* New York: Springer Publishing Co.

Linn, Margaret W., Joan S. Carmichael, Patricia Klitenick, Nancy Webb, and Lee Gurel. 1978. "Fertility Related Attitudes of Minority Mothers with Large and Small Families." *Journal of Applied Social Psychology* 8(1): 1-14.

Loken, Barbara and Martin Fishbein. 1980. "An Analysis of the Effects of Occupational Variables on Childbearing Intentions." *Journal of Applied Social Psychology* 10(3): 202–23.

Long, Larry and Diana De Are. 1981. "The Suburbanization of Blacks." *American Demographics* 3(8) September: 16–21,44.

McAdoo, Harriette. 1983. "Extended Family Support of Single Black Mothers." Final Report. National Institute of Mental Health.

——. 1982. "Stress Absorbing Systems in Black Families." *Family Relations* 31(October): 479–88.

——. 1981. "Youth, School and the Family in Transition." *Urban Education* 16(October): 261–77.

McAnarney, Elizabeth. 1982. *Adolescent Pregnancy: Psychological and Social Antecedents and Prevention.* Rochester: University of Rochester Medical Center.

McCarthy, James. 1979. "Religious Commitment, Affiliation and Marriage Dissolution." In R. Wuthnow, ed., *The Religious Dimension.* New York: Academic Press.

McCary, James L. 1978. *McCary's Human Sexuality,* 3rd ed. New York: D. Van Nostrand.

McGee, Elizabeth A. 1982. "Too Little, Too Late: Services for Teenage Parents," New York: Ford Foundation.

——. 1982. "Teenage Parents—Causes and Consequences." *New Generation* 62(3): Fall.

McKinney, Kathleen, Susan Sprecher, and John De Lamater. 1981. "The Self and Contraceptive Behavior." The University of Wisconsin, Center for Demographic and Ecology, Working Paper 81-37.

McLaughlin, Steven. 1981. "Educational and Occupational Aspirations and Determinants of Adolescent Fertility." Final Report to the National Institute of Child Health and Human Development. Seattle: Battelle Human Affairs Research Centers.

———. 1977. "Consequences of Adolescent Childbearing for the Mother's Occupational Attainment." Final Report to the National Institute of Child Health and Human Development. Seattle: Battelle Human Affairs Research Centers.

McLaughlin, Steven, and Michael Micklin. 1983. "The Timing of the First Birth and Changes in Personal Efficacy." *The Journal of Marriage and the Family* 45 (February): 47–55.

Macke, Anne and William Morgan. 1978. "Maternal Employment, Race, and Work Orientation of High School Girls," *Social Forces* 57: 187–204.

Mallar, Charles, Stuart Kerachsky, Craig Thornton, Michael Donihue, Carol Jones, David Long, Emmanuel Noggoh, and Jennifer Schore. 1980. "The Lasting Impacts of Job Corps Participation." *Youth Knowledge Development Report 3.4*, Princeton: Mathematica Policy Research.

Marecek, Jeanne. 1981. Presentation at Psycho-Social Workshop. Annual meetings of the Population Association of America, Washington, D.C.

Marin, Gerardo, Barbara Van Oss Marin, and Amado Padella. 1981. "The Meaning of Children for Hispanic Women." Paper presented at the meetings of the American Psychological Association. Los Angeles: University of California.

Marini, Margaret Mooney. 1978. "Sex Differences in the Determination of Adolescent Aspirations: A Review Research." *Sex Roles* 4(5): 723–53.

Marshall, Kimball, and Arthur Cosby. 1977. "Antecedents of Early Marital and Fertility Behavior." *Youth and Society* 9(2): 191–212.

Maslack, Germaine, and Graham Kerr. 1983. "Tailoring Sex-Education Programs to Adolescents—A Strategy for the Primary Prevention of Unwanted Adolescent Pregnancies." *Adolescence* 18: (Summer) 449–56.

Meara, Hannah. 1981. "Cognitive and Interactive Processes Among Never-Married Female and Male Partners." Presentation at the NICHD Contractor/Grantee Workshop on Adolescent Pregnancy and Childbearing, June 29–30.

Menken, Jane, and Ulla Larsen. 1983. "Age and Fertility: How Late Can You Wait?" Paper presented at the Annual Meetings of the Population Association of America.

Messaris, Paul, and Robert Hornik. 1983. "Work Status, Television Exposure and Educational Outcomes." In Cheryl Hayes and Sheila Kamerman, eds., *Children of Working Parents: Experiences and Outcomes*. Washington, D.C.: National Academy Press.

Michael, Robert T., and Nancy Brandon Tuma. 1982. "Employment, Unemployment, Schooling, Marriage, and Fertility Patterns of American Youths." National Opinion Research Center (July): 82–85.

Miller, Patricia, and William Simon. 1980. "The Development of Sexuality in Adolescence." In J. Adelson (ed.) *Handbook of Adolescent Psychology*. New York: John Wiley and Sons.

——. 1974. "Adolescent Sexual Behavior: Content and Change." *Social Problems* 22: 58–76.

Miller, Shelby. 1983. *Children and Parents: A Final Report*. New York: Child Welfare League of America.

Miller, Warren B. 1976. "Sexual and Contraceptive Behavior in Young Unmarried Women." *Primary Care*. (Fall/Winter): 427–53.

Millman, Sara, and Gerry Hendershot. 1980. "Early Fertility." *Family Planning Perspectives* 12(May/June): 139–49.

Mindick, Burton, and Stuart Oskamp. 1980. "Contraception Use Effectiveness: The Fit between Method and User Characteristics." Final Report to Center for Population Research, the National Institute of Child Health and Human Development for Contract Number 1-HD-82842.

Moore, Kristin A. 1980. "Policy Determinants of Teenage Childbearing." Final Report to the National Institute of Child Health and Human Development. Washington, D.C.: The Urban Institute.

——. 1978. "Teenage Childbirth and Welfare Dependency." *Family Planning Perspectives* 10 (July/August): 233–35.

Moore, Kristin A., James Peterson, and Frank Furstenburg. 1984. "Starting Early: The Antecedents of Early, Premarital Intercourse." Revised version of a paper presented at the meetings of the Population Association of America, Minneapolis, Minnesota.

Moore, Kristin A., and Martha Burt. 1982. *Private Crisis, Public Cost: Policy Perspectives on Teenage Childbearing*. Washington, D.C.: The Urban Institute.

Moore, Kristin A., and Linda Waite. 1981. "Marital Dissolution, Early Motherhood and Early Marriage." *Social Forces* 60(1): 20–40.

Moore, Kristin A., and Sandra Hofferth. 1980. "Factors Affecting Early Family Formation: A Path Model." *Population and Environment* 3(1): 73–96.

Moore, Kristin A., Linda Waite, Steven Caldwell, and Sandra Hofferth. 1978. "The Consequences of Age at First Childbirth: Educational Attainment." Working Paper 1146-01. Washington, D.C.: The Urban Institute.

Moore, Kristin A., and Sandra L. Hofferth. 1978. "The Consequences of Age at First Childbirth: Family Size." Working Paper 1146-02, Washington, D.C.: The Urban Institute.

Moore, Kristin A., and Steven B. Caldwell. 1977. "The Effect of Government Policies on Out-of-Wedlock Sex and Pregnancy." *Family Planning Perspectives* 9(July/August): 164-69.

Mosher, William. 1982. "Fertility and Family Planning in the 1970s: The National Survey of Family Growth." *Family Planning Perspectives* 14, (November/December): 314–20.

Mott, Frank L., ed. 1981. *Years for Decision: A Longitudinal Study of the Educational Labor Market, and Family Experiences of Young Women, 1968 to 1978*. Report submitted to U.S. Department of Labor. Cambridge: MIT Press.

Mott, Frank L., and Sylvia Moore. 1983. "The Tempo of Remarriage Among Young American Women." *Journal of Marriage and the Family* 45(2) May.

Mott, Frank L., and Nan L. Maxwell. 1981. "School-Age Mothers: 1968 and 1979." *Family Planning Perspectives* 6(November/December): 287–92.

Mott, Frank L., and Lois B. Shaw. 1978. *Work and Family in the School Leaving Years: A Comparison of Female High School Graduates and Dropouts.* Washington: Employment and Training Administration.

Namerow, Pearila, Susan Philliber, and Marilyn Hughes. 1983. "Follow-Up of Adolescent Family Planning Clinic Users." *Family Planning Perspectives* 15:172–76.

Nathanson, Constance, and Marshall Becker. 1983. "Aspirations, Opportunity Structures, and Reproductive Roles as Determinants of Contraceptive Behavior Among Adolescent Girls." Paper presented at the annual meetings of the Population Association of America.

National Assessment of Educational Progress. 1981. "Three National Assessments of Reading: Changes in Performance, 1970–80." Denver, Colo.: Education Commission of the States.

National Center for Education Statistics. 1982. *The Condition of Education: 1982.* Washington, D.C.: U.S. Government Printing Office.

——. 1979. *Digest of Educational Statistics: 1979.* Washington, D.C.: U.S. Government Printing Office.

National Center for Health Statistics. 1982. "Basic Data on Women Who Use Family Planning Clinics: United States, 1980." Data from the National Health Survey, Series 13, No. 67. Hyattsville, Md: Public Health Service, Department of Health and Human Services.

——. 1982. "Advance Report of Final Natality Statistics, 1980." *Monthly Vital Statistics Report*, 31, (8), Supplement.

——. 1981a. "Advance Report of Final Natality Statistics, 1981." *Monthly Vital Statistics Report*, 32(9), Supplement.

——. 1981b. "Interval Between Births: United States, 1970–77." *Monthly Vital Statistics Report* Series 21, No. 39.

——. 1981c. "Teenagers Who Use Organized Family Family Services: United States, 1978," *Monthly Vital Statistics Report* Series 13, No. 57.

Nelson, Kathleen, D. Key, J. Fletcher, E. Kirkpatrick, and R. Feinstein. 1982. "The Teen-Tot Clinic." *Journal of Adolescent Health Care* 3:19–23.

Newcomer, Susan, J. Richard Udry, and Freda Cameron. forthcoming. "Adolescent Sexual Behavior and Popularity." *Journal of Adolescence.*

Norton, Eleanor Holmes. 1983. "Children Having Children: Black Women Respond." Remarks at a Conference on Teenage Pregnancy, Washington, D.C.

O'Connell, Martin, and Carolyn Rodgers. 1984. "Out-of-Wedlock Births, Premarital Pregnancies, and their Effect on Family Formation and Dissolution." *Family Planning Perspectives* 16(4): 157–62.

——. 1982. "Out-of-Wedlock Childbearing: Trends and Differentials." Bureau of the Census, unpublished paper.

O'Connell, Martin, and Maurice J. Moore. 1980. "The Legitimacy Status of First Births to U.S. Women Aged 15–24, 1939–1978." *Family Planning Perspectives* 12 (January/February): 16–25.

O'Neill, June, and Rachel Braun. 1981. "Women and the Labor Market: A Survey of Issues and Policies in the United States." Washington, D.C.: The Urban Institute.

Orr, Margaret Terry. 1981. "Sex Education and Contraceptive Education in U.S. Public High Schools." *Family Planning Perspectives* 14(6): 304–13.

Ory, Howard. 1983. "Mortality Associated with Fertility and Fertility Control: 1983." *Family Planning Perspectives* 15(2): 57–63.

Parcel, Guy S., and Dave Luttman. 1981. "Evaluation of a Sex Education Course for Young Adolescents." *Family Relations* 30(1): 55–60.

Pearce, Diana, and Harriette McAdoo. 1981. "Women and Children: Alone and in Poverty." Washington, D.C.: National Advisory Council on Economic Opportunity.

Pedersen, Frank, Judith Rubenstein, and Leon Yarrow. 1979. "Infant Development in Father Absent Families." *The Journal of Genetic Psychology* 135: 51–61.

Peterson, James, and Nicholas Zill. 1983. "Marital Disruption, Parent/Child Relationships, and Behavioral Problems in Children." Revised version of paper presented at the annual meetings of the Society for Research in Child Development. Washington, D.C.: Child Trends, Inc.

Philliber, Susan G. 1982. "Staffing a Contraceptive Service for Adolescents: The Importance of Sex, Race, and Age." *Public Health Reports* March-April 97(2): 165–69.

Philliber, Susan G. and Pearila B. Namerow. 1983. "A Comparison of Responses to Adolescent-Oriented and Traditional Contraceptive Programs." *Journal of Ambulatory Care Management* (May): 32–42.

Philliber, Susan and Judith Jones. 1982. "Staffing a Contraceptive Service for Adolescents: the Importance of Sex, Race and Age." *Public Health Reports* 97(2): 165–69.

Piaget, J. "The Intellectual Development of the Adolescent." In G. Caplan and S. Lebovici, eds., *Adolescence: Psychosocial Perspectives*. New York: Basic Books.

Poland, M.L. and G.E. Beane. 1980. "A Study of the Effects of Folklore about the Body on IUD Use by Black American Adolescents." *Contraceptive Delivery Systems*: 1:333–40.

Polich, J. Michael, Phyllis Ellickson, Peter Reuter, and James Kahan. 1984. *Strategies for Controlling Adolescent Drug Use*. Santa Monica, Calif.: The Rand Corporation.

Polit, Denise F., Janet R. Kahn, Charles A. Murray, and Kevin W. Smith. *Needs and Characteristics of Pregnant and Parenting Teens: Baseline Report for Project Reaction*. New York: Manpower Development Research Corportation.

Pope, Hallowell. 1969. "Negro-White Differences in Decisions Regarding Illegitimate Children." *Journal of Marriage and the Family* (November): 756–64.

Pratt, L., and P. Whelpton. 1956. "Social and Psychological Factors Affecting Fertility." *Milbank Memorial Fund Quarterly* 34.

Presser, Harriet. 1978. "Age at Menarche, Socio-Sexual Behavior, and Fertility." *Social Biology* 25 (Summer): 94–101.

——. 1974. "Early Motherhood: Ignorance or Bliss?" *Family Planning Perspectives* 6(1): 8–14.

Quarm, Daisy. forthcoming. "Race Differences in Conjugal Power Structure: An Empirical Challenge to the Black Matriarchy Hypothesis." *Social Science Quarterly*.

Rains, Prudence. 1971. *Becoming an Unwed Mother*. Chicago: Aldine Atherton.

Reichelt, Paul, and Harriet Werley. 1976. "Sex Knowledge of Teenagers and the Effect of an Educational Rap Session." *Journal of Research and Development in Education* 10(1): 13–22.

Rickels, Karl. 1983. "A Study of Unwanted Pregnancy in Adolescents." Progress Report to the Public Health Service.

Ridley, J.S. 1959. "Number of Children Expected in Relation to Non-Familial Activities of the Wife." *Milbank Memorial Fund Quarterly* 37: 227–96.

Rindfuss, Ronald, and Craig St. John. 1983. "Social Determinants of Age at First Birth." *Journal of Marriage and the Family* 45(3): 553–65.

Rindfuss, Ronald, Larry Bumpass, and Craig St. John. 1980. "Education and Fertility: Implications for the Roles Women Occupy." *American Sociological Review* 45(3): 431–47.

Rivara, Frederick, Patrick Sweeney, and Brady Henderson. forthcoming. "A Case-Comparison Study of Teenage Fathers and Their Non-Father Peers." *Pediatrics*.

Roderick, Roger D. 1974. *Years for Decision: A Longitudinal Study of the Educational and Labor Market Experiences of Young Women*, Vol. 2. Washington, D.C.: U.S. Government Printing Office.

Rodick, J. Douglas and Scott W. Henggeler. 1980. "The Short-Term and Long-Term Amelioration of Academic and Motivational Deficiencies among Low-achieving Inner-City Adolescents." *Child Development* 51: 1126–32.

Rogers, Joseph, John Billy, and J. Richard Udry. 1982. "The Recession of Behaviors: Inconsistent Responses in Adolescent Sexuality Data." *Social Science Research* 11: 280–96.

Rooks, Evelyn, and Karl King. 1973. "A Study of the Marriage Role Expectations of Black Adolescents." *Adolescence* 8, (Fall): 317–24.

Roper, Brent, Linda Heath and Charles King. 1978. "Racial Consciousness: A New Guise for Traditionalism?" *Sociology and Social Research* 62(3): 431–47.

Rosen, Bernard C., and Carol S. Aneshensel. 1978. "Sex Differences in the Educational-Occupational Expectation Process." *Social Forces* 57 (September): 164–86.

Ross, Susan. 1979. *The Youth Values Project*. Washington, D.C.: The Population Institute.

Rothenberg, P.B., and S.G. Philliber. 1983. "Attitudes Toward Sex Education Among Black, Hispanic and White Inner-City Residents." *International Quarterly of Community Health Education*. 3(3): 291–99.

Rothenberg, Pearila Brickner. 1980. "Communication About Sex and Birth Control between Mothers and Their Adolescent Children." *Population and Environment* 3 (Spring): 35–50.

Roylance, Susan. 1981. Testimony presented to the Senate Committee on Labor and Human Resources, April 5.

Rumberger, Russell W. 1982. "Recent High School and College Experiences of Youth: Variations by Race, Sex, and Social Class." *Youth and Society* 13 (June): 449–70.

Rumberger, Russell. 1981. "Dropping Out of High School: The Influence of Race, Sex, and Family Background." Paper presented at the American Education Research Association meetings, Los Angeles.

Russo, Nancy, and Yvonne Brackbill. 1973. "Population and Youth." In James Fawcett ed. *Psychological Perspectives on Population*, New York: Basic Books, pp. 393–427.

Ryder, Norman, and Charles Westoff. 1972. "Wanted and Unwanted Fertility in the United States: 1965 and 1970." In Commission on Population Growth and the American Future. *Demographic and Social Aspects of Population Growth*, C. Westoff and R. Parke ed. Washington, D.C.: Government Printing Office.

Sandell, Steven H., and David Shapiro. 1980. "Work Expectations, Human Capital Accumulation, and the Wages of Young Women." *Journal of Human Resources* 15(3): 335–53.

Saucier, Jean-Francois, and Anne-Marie Ambert. 1983. "Parental Marital Status and Adolescents' Health-Risk Behavior." *Adolescence* 18(70) Summer: 403–11.

Scales, Peter, and Douglas Kirby. 1981. "A Review of Exemplary Sex Education Programs for Teenagers Offered by Nonschool Organizations." *Family Relations* 30(2): 238–246.

Scheirer, Mary Ann, Thomas Dial, and Ann White. 1982. "The Relationships of Mother's Age at First Birth to Public Assistance." Final Report to the National Institute of Child Health and Human Development.

Schinke, Steven, and Lewayne Gilchrist. 1984. *Life Skills Counseling with Adolescents*. Baltimore, Md: University Park Press.

Schinke, Steven, Betty Blythe, Lewayne Gilchrist, and Gloria Burt. 1981. "Primary Prevention of Adolescent Pregnancy." *Social Work with Groups* 4: 121–35.

Schinke, Steven, Lewayne Gilchrist, and Richard Small. 1979. "Preventing Unwanted Adolescent Pregnancy: A Cognitive-Behavioral Approach." *American Journal of Orthopsychiatry* 49(1): 81–88.

Segal, Steven, and Joseph DuCette. 1973. "Locus of Control and Premarital High School Pregnancy." *Psychological Reports* 33: 887–90.

Select Committee on Children, Youth and Families, U.S. House of Representatives. 1983. "U.S. Children and Their Families: Current Conditions and Recent Trends."

Shaw, Lois B. 1982. "High School Completion for Young Women: Effects of Low Income and Living with a Single Parent." *Journal of Family Issues* 3(June): 147–63.

Shea, John R. 1971. *Years for Decision: A Longitudinal Study of the Educational and Labor Market Experience of Young Women*, vol. 1. Washington, D.C.: U.S. Government Printing Office.

Shirm, Allen, James Trussell, Jane Menken and William Grady. 1982. "Contraceptive Failure in the United States: The Impact of Social, Economic and Demographic Factors." *Family Planning Perspectives* 14 (March/April): 68–75.

Simms, Margaret C., and M. Laurie Leitch. 1983. "Determinants of Youth Participation in Employment and Training Programs with a Special Focus on Young Women." Washington, D.C.: The Urban Institute.

Smith, Elsie J. 1982. "The Black Female Adolescent: A Review of the Educational Career and Psychological Literature." *Psychology of Women Quarterly* 6(Spring): 261–88.

Smith-Lovin, Lynn, and Ann Tickamyer. 1978. "Nonrecursive Models of Labor Force Participation: Insights from Nonrecursive Models." *American Sociological Review* 43(4): 541–57.

Sonenstein, Freya, and Karen Pittman. 1984. "The Availability of Sex Education in Large City School Districts." *Family Planning Perspectives* 16 (January/February): 19–25.

———. 1983. "The What and Why of Sex Education: Describing and Explaining Program Content and Coverage in City School Districts." Washington, D.C.: The Urban Institute.

Spitze, Glenna. 1978. "Role Experiences of Young Women: A Longitudinal Test of the Role Hiatus Hypothesis." *Journal of Marriage and the Family* 40(3): 471–79.

SRI International. 1983. *Final Report of the Seattle-Denver Income Maintenance Experiment.* Menlo Park, California: SRI International.

Stack, Carol B. 1974. *All Our Kin—Strategies for Survival in a Black Community.* New York: Harper & Row.

Steinlauf, Barbara. 1979. "Problem-solving Skills, Locus of Control, and the Contraceptive Effectiveness of Young Women." *Child Development* 50: 268–271.

Stolzenberg, Ross, and Linda Waite. 1977. "Fertility Expectations and Plans for Employment." *American Sociological Review* 42: 769–783.

Sweet, James. 1982. "Work and Fertility." In G. Fox, ed., *The Childbearing Decision.* Beverly Hills: Sage, 197–218.

———. 1982. "Components of Change in the Number of Black Households: 1970–1980." Working Paper 82-55, Center for Demography and Ecology, University of Wisconsin.

———. 1979. "Changes in the Allocation of Time of Young Black Women Among Schooling, Marriage, Work and Childrearing: 1960–1976." Working Paper 79-31, Center for Demography and Ecology, University of Wisconsin.

———. 1973. *Women in the Labor Force.* New York: Academic Press.

Thomson, Elizabeth, Andrew Davidson, and Richard Williams. 1982. "Measurement Models for the Subjective Utility of Children." Working Paper 82-11, University of Wisconsin, Center for Demography and Ecology.

Thornton, Arland. 1983. Presentation at a Workshop on Household Structure. Bethesda, Md: Center for Population Research, NICHD.

Thorpe, Clairburne. 1972. "Social Status and the Pill at a Black Woman's College." *College Student Journal* 6(2) April: 66–73.

Tittle, Carol Kehr. 1981. *Careers and Family: Sex Roles and Adolescent Life Plans.* Los Angeles: Sage Library of Social Research.

Trussell, T. James, Jane Menken, Barbara Lindheim, and Barbara Vaughan. 1980. "The Impact of Restricting Medicaid Financing of Abortion." *Family Planning Perspectives* 12(May/June): 120–30.

Trussell, James and Jane Menken. 1978. "Early Childbearing and Subsequent Fertility." *Family Planning Perspectives* 10 (July/August): 209–18.

Turner, Castellano, and William Darity. 1971. "Attitudes toward Family Planning and Fears of Genocide as a Function of Race Consciousness." Paper presented at the Midwestern Psychological Association meetings, Detroit, Michigan.

Uhlenberg, Peter. 1973. "Fertility Patterns within the Mexican-American Population." *Social Biology* 20(1): 30–39.

U.S. Department of Commerce, Bureau of the Census. 1983a. *America's Black Population: 1970 to 1982.* Special Publication PIO/POP-83-1. Washington, D.C.: U.S. Government Printing Office.

———. 1983b. *Fertility of American Women: June 1981.* Current Population Reports. Series P-20, No. 378. Washington, D.C.: U.S. Government Printing Office.

———. 1983c. *School Enrollment—Social and Economic Characteristics of Students: October 1981* (Advance Report), P-20, No. 373. Washington, D.C.: U.S. Government Printing Office.

———. 1982. *Fertility of American Women: June 1980.* Current Population Reports, Series P-20, No. 375. Washington, D.C.: U.S. Government Printing Office.

———. 1981. *School Enrollment—Social and Economic Characteristics of Students: October 1979.* Current Population Reports, P-20, No. 360. Washington, D.C.: U.S. Government Printing Office.

———. 1980. *Families Maintained by Female Householders: 1970-79.* Current Population Reports, P-23, No. 107. Washington, D.C.: U.S. Government Printing Office.

———. 1972. *School Enrollment—Social and Economic Characteristics of Students: October 1971.* Current Population Reports, P-20, No. 241. Washington, D.C.: Government Printing Office.

Ventura, Stephanie. 1980. "Trends and Differentials in Births to Unmarried Women: United States, 1970–76." Vital and Health Statistics, Series 21, Data from the National Vital Statistics System; No. 36. Washington, D.C.: U.S. Government Printing Office.

Vincenzi, Harry and Jeanette Brewe. 1982. "The Education Performance of Children of Teenage Mothers." Paper presented at the Annual Conference of the American Educational Research Association.

Waite, Linda J., and Glenna D. Spitze. 1981. "Young Women's Transition to Marriage." *Demography* 18(November): 681–94.

Waite, Linda J., and Kristin A. Moore. 1978. "The Impact of an Early First Birth on Young Women's Educational Attainment." *Social Forces* 56 March: 845–65.

Waite, Linda J., and Ross Stolzenberg. 1976. "Intended Childbearing and Labor Force Participation of Young Women: Insights from Nonrecursive Models." *American Sociological Review* 41(2): 235–52.

Warwick, Donald, and Nancy Williamson. 1972. "Population Policy and Spanish-Surname Americans." In Veatch, Robert ed., *Population Policy and Ethics-The American Experience.* New York. Irvington Publishers.

Weisbord, Robert. 1973. "Birth Control and the Black American: A Matter of Genocide?" *Demography* 10(4): 571–90.

Weiss, Robert. 1984. "The Impact of Marital Dissolution on Income and Consumption in Single-Parent Households." *Journal of Marriage and Family Review* 46(1): 115–27.

Weller, Robert. 1979. "The Differential Attainment of Family Size Goals by Race." *Population Studies* 33(1): 157–64.

———. 1976. "Number and Timing Failures Among Legitimate Births in the United States: 1968, 1969 and 1972." *Family Planning Perspectives* 8 (May/June): 111–16.

Wertheimer, Richard, and Kristin A. Moore. 1982. "Teenage Childbearing: Public Sector Costs." Final Report to the National Institute of Child Health and Human Development.

Westoff, Charles, Gerard Cabot, and Andrew Foster. 1983. "Teenage Fertility in Developed Nations: 1971–1980." *Family Planning Perspectives* 15(3): 105–10.

Westoff, Charles, and Norman Ryder. 1971. *Reproduction in the United States.* Princeton: Princeton University Press.

Whelpton, Pascal K., Arthur A. Campbell, and John E. Patterson. 1966. *Fertility and Family Planning in the United States.* Princeton: Princeton University Press.

White, C.D. 1974. "The Social Mobility-Fertility Hypothesis: A Racial and Class Comparison Among Southern Females." Texas A & M University, College Station, Texas Agricultural Experiment Station.

White, Lynn. 1981. "A Note on Racial Differences in the Effect of Female Economic Opportunity on Marriage Rate." *Demography* 18(3): 349–54.

———. 1979. "The Correlates of Urban Illegitimacy in the United States, 1960–1970." *Journal of Marriage and the Family* 41: 715–26.

Wilkinson, Charles B., and William A. O'Connor. 1977. "Growing Up Male in a Black Single-Parent Family." *Psychiatric Annals* 7(July): 50–59.

Williams, Paul R. 1977. "Black Illegitimacy and Social Response." Unpublished Paper.

Zabin, Laurie Schwab. 1983a. Workshop on Adolescent Pregnancy. Center for Population Research, National Institute of Child Health and Human Development.

Zabin, Laurie Schwab, and Samuel Clark. 1983. "Institutional Factors Affecting Teenagers' Choice and Reasons for Delay in Attending a Family Planning Clinic." *Family Planning Perspectives* 15(1): 25–29.

Zabin, Laurie Schwab. 1981. "The Impact of Early Use of Prescription Contraceptives on Reducing Premarital Teenage Pregnancies." *Family Planning Perspectives* 13(2): 72.

Zelnik, Melvin. 1979. "Sex Education and Knowledge of Pregnancy Risk among U.S. Teenage Women." *Family Planning Perspectives* 11(6): 355–57.

Zelnik, Melvin, and Farida Shah. 1983. "First Intercourse Among Young Americans." *Family Planning Perspectives* 15(2): 64–70.

Zelnik, Melvin, and Young Kim. 1982. "Sex Education and Its Association with Teenage Sexual Activity, Pregnancy and Contraceptive Use." *Family Planning Perspectives* 14(3): 117–26.

Zelnik, Melvin, John Kantner, and Kathleen Ford. 1981. *Sex and Pregnancy in Adolescence*. Beverly Hills: Sage.

Zelnik, Melvin, and John F. Kantner. 1981. "Contraceptive Patterns and Premarital Pregnancy Among Women Aged 15–19 in 1976." In F. Furstenberg, R. Lincoln., and J. Menken, eds., *Teenage Sexuality, Pregnancy and Childbearing*. New York: Alan Guttmacher Institute.

———. 1980. "Sexual Activity, Contraceptive Use and Pregnancy Among Metropolitan-Area Teenagers: 1971–1979." *Family Planning Perspectives* 12(September/October): 230–37.

Zill, Nicholas. forthcoming. *American Children: Happy, Healthy and Insecure*.

Zill, Nicholas and James Peterson. 1981. "Television Viewing in the United States and Children's Intellectual, Social and Emotional Development." *Television and Children* 4(2): 21–27.

Index

Abortion: and age, 59, 60–64; availability of, services, 47–49, 62, 64; conclusions about, 65, 131–32; and married women, 60–61; and medicaid, 62, 64; and nonmarital childbearing, 60–61; and race, 60, 61–62, 65; rate, 21–22, 22–23, 59–62; teenage parenthood and, 22–23
Accessibility of birth control, 47–48, 49–59
Adolescent Pregnancy Programs, Office of (OAPP), 98, 100
Adoption and nonmarital childbearing, 24
AFDC (Aid to Families with Dependent Children), 1, 96
Age: and abortions, 59, 60–64; and contraceptive use, 51–52, 65; and family planning services, 49, 50; and attitudes about marriage, 115–17; and marriage patterns, 103–7, 109; and sex education, 35, 44; and subsequent childbearing, 25–26
Aspirations. *See* Expectations
Attainment, educational; and educational expectations, 78–83; and fertility, 68; and income, 74–75, 81; and race, 68, 74–76, 78–83, 84–86; and sex education, 35
Attitudes: and age, 115–17; about birth control, 35–37; and childbearing, 115–19; conclusions about, 128–31; and marriage patterns, 107, 115–19; about marriage, 35–37, 115–19

Ballard, Charles, 122–23
Birth control, 47–59: accessibility of, 47–48, 49–59; availability of, 47–49; and barrier analogy, 40–41, 47; cost of, 53; discussion about, 58–59; and fecundity, 56; information about, 33, 36; prescription/nonprescription, 52–53; and sexual activity, 54, 56; teenagers' attitudes about,

35–37; teenagers' knowledge about, 31–35, 41–44. *See also* Contraception; Contraceptive services
Burt, Martha, 47, 110

Carlson, Elwood, 109, 110
CETA, 97–98
Cherlin, Andrew, 90, 107
Childbearing: and abortions, 60–61; and age, 25–26; conclusions about, 127; and family structure, 120, 122; and fertility, 9–11; and income, 16–17, 120–21; and attitudes about marriage, 115–19; nonmarital, 11–17, 24, 29n2, 60–61, 103, 117–19; of separated women, 29n2; subsequent, 24–26; teenage, 1, 9–11, 24–26, 127
Clark, Samuel, 34–35, 59
Clinics. *See* Family planning services
Cognitive maturity and sex education, 34, 44–45, 94
Conclusions: about abortions, 65, 131–32; about attitudes, 128–31; about contraception, 64–65, 131–32; about education, 83–86, 132–34; about employment, 100–101, 134–35; about fertility, 26–27, 127; about information, 44–45, 128–31; about job training, 101, 134–35; about marriage and family, 123–24, 135–37; about sex education, 44–45, 129; about teenage childbearing, 26–27, 127; overall, 138–39
Contraception, 47–59, 64–65; conclusions about, 64–65, 131–32; discussion about, 58–59; and nonsupply factors, 53–57, 58–59; and supply factors, 49–53, 58–59. *See also* Birth control
Contraceptive services: availability of, 48–49, 49–59; accessibility of, 47–59; age

161